Autism

LIVING WITH A SPECIAL NEED

Attention-Deficit/Hyperactivity Disorder

Autism

Blindness and Vision Impairment

Brain Injury

Chronic Illness

Deaf and Hard of Hearing

Emotional Disturbance

Gender Issues

Intellectual Disabilities

Learning Disabilities

Physical Challenges

Protective Services

Speech Impairment

The Foster Care System

The Juvenile Court System

The Laws That Protect Youth with Special Needs

LIVING WITH A SPECIAL NEED

Autism

BY SHERRY BONNICE

MASON CREST

Mason Crest
450 Parkway Drive, Suite D
Broomall, PA 19008
www.masoncrest.com

Printed in the United States of America.

Series ISBN: 978-1-4222-3027-5
ISBN: 978-1-4222-3029-9
ebook ISBN: 978-1-4222-8814-6

Library of Congress Cataloging-in-Publication Data

Bonnice, Sherry, 1956-
  [Hidden child]
  Autism / by Sherry Bonnice.
    pages cm. — (Living with a special need)
  Previously published as: The hidden child, [2004].
  Includes glossary.
  Includes bibliographical references and index.
  Audience: Grade 7-8
  ISBN 978-1-4222-3029-9 (hardback) — ISBN 978-1-4222-3027-5 (series) — ISBN 978-1-4222-8814-6 (ebook) 1. Autistic children—Juvenile literature. 2. Autism in children—Juvenile literature. I. Title.
  RJ506.A9B657 2014
  618.92'85882—dc23
                        2014010622

Picture credits: Benjamin Stewart: pp. 51, 63, 115; Comstock: pp. 23, 35, 69, 117; Corel: pp. 49, 80, 82; Life Art: pp. 21, 37, 97, 107; Photo Alto: pp. 25, 40, 67, 71, 93, 106; PhotoDisc: pp. 19, 24, 26, 34, 36, 39, 54, 73, 79, 95, 104; Photo Spin: pp. 68, 91, 94, 116; Research Foundation/Camp Abilities: p. 65. Individuals in Corel, Photo Alto, PhotoDisc, and Photo Spin images are models, and the images are intended for illustrative purposes only.

Contents

KEY ICONS TO LOOK FOR:

Text-Dependent Questions: These questions send the reader back to the text for more careful attention to the evidence presented there.

Words to Understand: These words with their easy-to-understand definitions will increase the reader's understanding of the text, while building vocabulary skills.

Series Glossary of Key Terms: This back-of-the book glossary contains terminology used throughout this series. Words found here increase the reader's ability to read and comprehend higher-level books and articles in this field.

Research Projects: Readers are pointed toward areas of further inquiry connected to each chapter. Suggestions are provided for projects that encourage deeper research and analysis.

Sidebars: This boxed material within the main text allows readers to build knowledge, gain insights, explore possibilities, and broaden their perspectives by weaving together additional information to provide realistic and holistic perspectives.

A child with special needs is not defined by his disability.
It is just one part of who he is.

INTRODUCTION

Each child is unique and wonderful. And some children have differences we call special needs. Special needs can mean many things. Sometimes children will learn differently, or hear with an aid, or read with Braille. A young person may have a hard time communicating or paying attention. A child can be born with a special need, or acquire it by an accident or through a health condition. Sometimes a child will be developing in a typical manner and then become delayed in that development. But whatever problems a child may have with her learning, emotions, behavior, or physical body, she is always a person first. She is not defined by her disability; instead, the disability is just one part of who she is.

Inclusion means that young people with and without special needs are together in the same settings. They learn together in school; they play together in their communities; they all have the same opportunities to belong. Children learn so much from each other. A child with a hearing impairment, for example, can teach another child a new way to communicate using sign language. Someone else who has a physical disability affecting his legs can show his friends how to play wheelchair basketball. Children with and without special needs can teach each other how to appreciate and celebrate their differences. They can also help each other discover how people are more alike than they are different. Understanding and appreciating how we all have similar needs helps us learn empathy and sensitivity.

In this series, you will read about young people with special needs from the unique perspectives of children and adolescents who are experiencing the disability firsthand. Of course, not all children with a particular disability are the same as the characters in the stories. But the stories demonstrate at an emotional level how a special need impacts a child, his family, and his friends. The factual material in each chapter will expand your horizons by adding to your knowledge about a particular disability. The series as a whole will help you understand differences better and appreciate how they make us all stronger and better.

—Cindy Croft
Educational Consultant

YOUTH WITH SPECIAL NEEDS provides a unique forum for demystifying a wide variety of childhood medical and developmental disabilities. Written to captivate an adolescent audience, the books bring to life the challenges and triumphs experienced by children with common chronic conditions such as hearing loss, intellectual disabilities, physical differences, and speech difficulties. The topics are addressed frankly through a blend of fiction and fact. Students and teachers alike can move beyond the information provided by accessing the resources offered at the end of each text.

This series is particularly important today as the number of children with special needs is on the rise. Over the last three decades, advances in pediatric medical techniques have allowed children who have chronic illnesses and disabilities to live longer, more functional lives. As a result, these children represent an increasingly visible part of North American population in all aspects of daily life. Students are exposed to peers with special needs in their classrooms, through extracurricular activities, and in the community. Often, young people have misperceptions and unanswered questions about a child's disabilities—and more important, his or her *abilities*. Many times, there is no vehicle for talking about these complex issues in a comfortable manner.

This series provides basic information that will leave readers with a deeper understanding of each condition, along with an awareness of some of the associated emotional impacts on affected children, their families, and their peers. It will also encourage further conversation about these issues. Most important, the series promotes a greater comfort for its readers as they live, play, and work side by side with these individuals who have medical and developmental differences—youth with special needs.

—Dr. Lisa Albers, Dr. Carolyn Bridgemohan, Dr. Laurie Glader
Medical Consultants

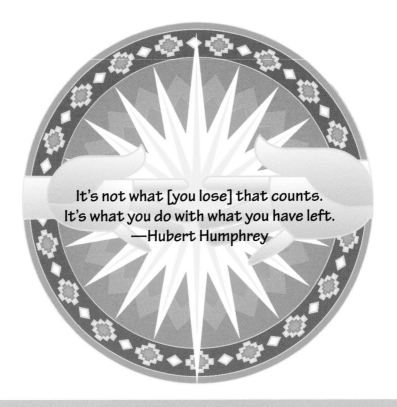

It's not what [you lose] that counts.
It's what you do with what you have left.
—Hubert Humphrey

Words to Understand

colic: A condition, seen often in babies, consisting of severe abdominal pain. Though uncomfortable, colic is rarely dangerous to babies experiencing it.

audiologist: A doctor who deals with the science of hearing.

neurodevelopment disorders: Disorders that occur in the brain and can affect a person's emotions and learning abilities.

monotone: Even, uniform, and without variation.

psychological: Relating to the mind or mental processes.

regress: Movement backward to a previous and especially worse or more primitive state or condition.

electrophysiological: Relating to electrical aspects of bodily functions. For example, an electrophysiological exam of the eye might examine the electrical impulses traveling and carrying messages between the brain and the eye.

1

LOSING TUCKER

Livie walked down the hall toward Tucker's room. When she reached the door, she leaned against the frame and watched her younger brother. He stood in the corner of his bedroom, facing a small wooden shelf. The shelves, painted his favorite color, turquoise, were lined with cups—Tucker's most precious collection. He held his favorite mug, etched in a deep metallic rust color with a sand-colored handle. The mug was one of Livie's favorites also.

The collection of cups included McDonald's and Dunkin' Donuts labels, as well as plastics of every size and color. In a funny way, the cups and mugs added to Tucker's personality. Livie enjoyed helping him learn colors using the plastic cups. Tucker was so grateful when she added to his collection. Whenever Livie and her mother cleaned the house, they found cups in the most unusual places, and they had many laughs over those finds. But Livie still wondered why Tucker had such a fascination with cups.

Deep down, Livie knew the answer to this question. Tucker had autism, and at age thirteen he still dealt with life on a different level than her friends' brothers and sisters. Although he went to her school, he didn't relate with people in the same way as she and her friends did. Of course, this meant Livie did not have to deal with a lot of arguing like other brothers and sisters or fighting over using the phone—Tucker didn't talk on the phone often. They didn't fight over whose job it was to clear the table because Tucker didn't try to get out of chores. His life was very structured and he knew what was expected of him each day. If he was supposed to take out the garbage, for example, he did. Everything was best if it stayed exactly the same.

Livie remembered when her mother told her she would have a new brother or sister. She was so excited; babies were one of her favorite things and now she would have one living in her house. One day Mom brought out Livie's baby clothes to wash any that could be used again. Livie loved hearing about the things she had worn on different occasions and dreaming of the new baby wearing them, too. Another time, her mother took her shopping to pick out a stuffed bear that would be a special gift to the baby from "Big Sister."

Born on a snowy day in March, Livie's baby brother was named Nathan Alexander Montgomery III. Livie gave her brother the little bear named Tucker Bear.

"Are you a little Tucker Bear, too?" Livie shook the little bear in front of the new baby. Soon everyone began calling him Tucker. Because Dad was called Nate and Grandpa Montgomery was Nathan, Tucker's nickname became an easy way to distinguish the Montgomery men. So Tucker became Tucker, right from the start.

Mom kept track of the major events of his first two years. She recorded his first smile, his first tooth, when he began crawling, and his first steps. Livie thought he was really fun when he began to talk. Short words, words that sounded like but weren't quite the words she and her parents used. Finally Tucker spoke in short phrases, like the day her mother made cookies and handed one to him.

"Two ones." Tucker smiled. They all laughed as Mom gave him a second cookie.

Livie recalled only a few of these bigger events until just before Tucker's second birthday. Life was fairly normal, but then things changed. Her parents began to notice that Tucker did not talk as often as he used to. He went from cute little phrases to saying only one word, then to words that sounded more like grunts, until finally he didn't speak at all. The family tried to lure him into talking by showing him some of his favorite toys or foods, things he had been naming only weeks earlier. But Tucker just stared into space.

Once they began worrying about his speech, Mom and Dad paid attention to how often Tucker cried compared to Livie when she was a baby. Tucker had always been a sensitive baby. At first, Livie's parents just thought it was temperament or **colic** or a busy schedule, but now it seemed as if they might have missed something that was wrong. More and more, he cried when anyone picked him up, even Mom and Dad. He seemed to like being alone, sitting in his corner.

Livie's parents even watched videos of Tucker to help them understand what was wrong. "Look how happy he seems sitting there watching the other children play. I never noticed that he didn't really join in much," Mom said.

"There's Livie pushing him on his little tricycle, back and forth, and he loves it. He's laughing."

"I never noticed him in the corner during Livie's last birthday party. He's just sitting there, turning his rattle over and over. In the Christmas video, he's just sitting there with that rattle. Nate, what do you think? Why is he so alone most of the time? How did we get to leaving him alone so much?"

Livie's father shook his head. "I think he's so much happier when we leave him alone and he doesn't cry so often, that we have just slowly adapted our care for him to meet his reaction to us."

"And now it's gotten to where he doesn't even want us to hold him. Do you think this is our fault? Haven't we given him enough attention?"

"I don't know, I just don't know."

One day after school Livie found her mother in her favorite chair in the family room. She just sat there crying and staring at Tucker. At first Livie's heart raced because her mother's staring reminded her so much of Tucker that Livie wondered if her mom had caught whatever it was that was wrong with Tucker.

Her mother looked up. "He's been in the corner holding that rattle, turning it around and around, then hitting it against his front teeth, then turning it around and around, then hitting his teeth. Again and again and again. It's been so awful. I tried to pick him up two different times—but if I even reached for him he began that terrible screaming, so I backed off. It's breaking my heart to let him just sit there." She started to cry again, and Livie cried too.

Tucker's second birthday was not as happy as his first. There were balloons, a cake, and presents. Grandma and Grandpa were there, and so were Livie's aunt, uncle, and cousins. But Tucker wasn't really there. He didn't look at anyone. He wouldn't blow out the candles or open presents. He just sat in his corner with one of his toys.

"I'm so glad I didn't invite any children," Mom said with a catch in her voice. "I couldn't stand to have their parents see him this way. I don't understand what's happening."

"What did the doctor say this week when you took Tucker for his two-year checkup?" Grandma asked.

"I told him some of the things we had been noticing, you know, how he likes to be alone so much, his fascination with that rattle, and how often he cries, as if just by touching him we were hurting him. The doctor didn't seem to think there was a problem." Mom wiped her eyes with a tissue. "It wasn't until I told him that Tucker just wouldn't talk at all anymore that the doctor became concerned. All those other things . . . but it was the talking that made a difference." Livie's mom walked to the corner where Tucker sat. "The doctor also said it could just be a phase Tucker's going through, but just to be sure, the doctor wants me to take Tucker to see an **audiologist** to have a hearing test."

"The doctor says it could be nothing," Livie's father put in, "but he thinks we need to be sure. And this is just a place to start. Besides, I'm sure his hearing is fine, Mandy. It's probably just like the doctor said—Tucker's going through a phase. You know, one of those two-year-old things."

"Well, now, let's just look for the best in this," Livie's tgrand-mother said. "We have so much to be thankful for and it is Tucker's second birthday. How about some more cake?"

Everyone tried to be happy the rest of the evening but Livie knew this was serious. While she and her cousins played in her room, Livie couldn't stop thinking about what was going on with Tucker. She felt a pain in her stomach.

During the next few weeks, Mom and Dad questioned every-one. They compared Tucker to every two-year-old they knew. Every time he did something different than other toddlers, Mom and Dad became more desperate. While talking on the phone, they frowned. When they tried to interact with Tucker, they looked sad. They al-most never laughed anymore. Livie felt like all the happy times were gone. What was wrong with Tucker? Why were her parents so scared?

Tucker continued to sit in his corner most of the time. He cried if Mom moved him. He hated loud noises. Sometimes even quiet talking seemed too loud for him. One night while Mom, Dad, and Livie sat in the family room playing a game, Tucker put his hands to his ears. Then he picked up his rattle and began turning it around in his hands and hitting it against his teeth. He always did that when he was upset. When Mom tried to stop him, Tucker cried. He rolled over on his side and curled up into a ball. The more Mom tried to comfort him, the louder he cried.

"Mandy, just leave him there," Dad said.

"I can't let him cry like this."

But Tucker screamed and pulled away. Mom ran from the room.

Dad looked at Livie. "Would you rather do something in your room? You don't have to stay here with me."

"I don't mind." Livie lied. She wanted to scream at Tucker and tell him to be quiet so they could all be happy again. Or even worse, she wanted to tell him to go somewhere else to live.

Later that night, Livie came down from her room because she couldn't sleep. Her stomach hurt and she wanted to tell her parents she was sorry for wishing Tucker would live somewhere else. But as she got to the bottom of the stairs, she heard her mother. "Nate, don't you understand? We've lost him. He's gone and we have to get him back."

"I know, I feel the same way, but you have to pace yourself. And there's still Livie to think about. Have you seen the way she looks at us lately? She probably wonders if we're going to be all right as much as we wonder what will happen to Tucker. She might not even like Tucker much right now. Or us."

Livie saw Mom lean over on Dad's shoulder, and they both began to cry. "I know. I'll try to get someone to come over so I can spend some time with her," Mom said.

Livie walked quietly back to her room. Tucker was lost and nobody knew what to do. She wondered where he went and if anyone could find him. Livie got under the covers and said her prayers again. "Please help Mom and Dad find Tucker, please."

WHAT IS AUTISM?

- According to the National Institutes of Health, autism is a range of complex **neurodevelopmental disorders**.
- Symptoms usually appear in children before the age of three, and some children with autism can seem to be developing normally until sometime between 18 and 24 months of age.
- Affected persons display impairment in social skills, imagination, activity, and language skills.
- Autism is a spectrum disorder. This means individuals not only have different symptoms from each other, but those symptoms also vary in intensity. One child may not be able to speak at all, another may speak using one or two words at a time, and another may seem fairly normal when he speaks except for a **monotone** presentation.
- Autism is not caused by **psychological** or emotional problems.
- It is four to five times more likely to occur in boys than in girls.
- Autism occurs around the world, affecting persons of all racial, ethnic, religious, and economic backgrounds.
- Some persons with autism are nonverbal, but others are able to speak and communicate more normally.
- In America, about one out of every 88 children has autism.
- Today, more people than ever before are being diagnosed with some form of autism.

Persons with autism may exhibit some of the following traits:

- resistance to change
- difficulty in expressing needs, using gestures or pointing instead of words
- repeating words or phrases instead of carrying on a two-way conversation
- laughing, crying, or other acting out for reasons unknown to others
- preferring to be alone; aloof manner
- tantrums
- difficulty in socializing with others
- may not want to cuddle or be cuddled
- little or no eye contact
- may be unresponsive to normal teaching methods
- odd play that may continue for hours at a time
- spins objects
- inappropriate attachments to objects
- over-sensitivity or under-sensitivity to pain that may cause reckless or annoying behavior
- no real fears of danger
- noticeable physical over-activity or extreme under-activity
- uneven gross/fine motor skills
- does not respond to name or being addressed personally, ignores persons and happenings within a room as if unable to hear what's going on around him

Language Skills

The parents of children with regressive autism usually notice a problem with language skills first. These children develop verbally and then appear to suddenly *regress*. Some retain a few words, but many lose all verbal skills.

A child with autism will lack communication skills.

Other children continue to communicate but do not gain any social skills while others never gain any language function. Between these two groups is a wide range of persons who use language in many different ways.

Many children with autism repeat words they hear, sometimes again and again. Others repeat verses of songs or poems over and over.

Children with autism often do not use the word "I." One child addressed her mother every time she had a need. "Mom, want a drink," she would say when she was thirsty.

Children often invent their own way of communicating, either using one word to mean a whole concept or task or by making up words of their own to share needs or thoughts.

AUTISM SCREENING AT WELL-CHILD DOCTOR VISITS

The American Academy of Pediatrics (AAP) recommends that developmental observation should be performed at all well-child visits from infancy through school-age, and at any age thereafter if concerns are raised about social acceptance, learning, or or behavior. The following is a list of milestones that normally occur during a child's development:

- babbling by twelve months
- gesturing (e.g., pointing, waving bye-bye) by twelve months
- single words by sixteen months
- two-word spontaneous phrases—not just repeated phrases—by twenty-four months

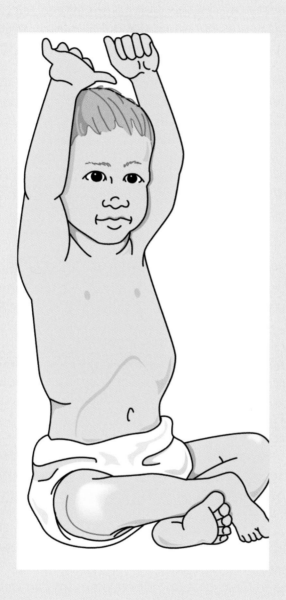

All babies pass through developmental stages.

Also recommended is that siblings of children diagnosed with autism be closely monitored not only for any evidence of autistic symptoms but also for language delays, learning difficulties, social problems, and anxiety or depressive symptoms.

The Modified Checklist for Autism in Toddlers (M-CHAT) or the Early Screening of Autistic Traits Questionnaire should be used to further evaluate anyone who fails to achieve the milestones listed above. Laboratory testing should include a hearing assessment and lead screening. Behavioral hearing should be measured along with middle ear function, and *electrophysiological* procedures should be performed.

M-CHAT

The M-CHAT should be conducted at each well-child checkup, and has been validated to screen toddlers between sixteen and thirty months old. It was created to replace the Checklist for Autism in Toddlers (CHAT), as well as to detect as many cases of autism as possible.

The M-CHAT only takes a few minutes to score, and a child that fails more than a total of three items or two items that are labeled "critical," are considered to be at risk of autism. However, because of the sensitivity of this screening, many children that do not have autism may score as being at risk of autism. This is why there is a second part to the M-CHAT: the follow-up interview, which is done with a healthcare provider. The healthcare provider asks a series of questions based on the answers to the M-CHAT, and if the child fails the follow-up interview, he is referred to a specialist for diagnosis. (The M-CHAT is a screening tool only, not a diagnostic test.)

Some children that do not have autism can still be labeled as at risk of autism after the follow-up interview, but these children could be at risk of other developmental disor-

ders, not just autism, so it is important that they are sent to a specialist.

THE HISTORY OF AUTISM

Autism was first described by Dr. Leo Kanner in 1943. He described the disorder as a narrowing of the person's sensory perceptions, including their relationships with people. The limited scope of the affected person was typically so extreme it eventually included no one else. The children Kanner studied would not involve themselves in the lives of others and rebelled against anyone interrupting their lives, including their own parents. Kanner noticed several things about these children:

A child with autism lives in his own small world.

A child with autism may be able to manipulate objects skillfully but still be unable to communicate with the world of other human beings.

- "The outstanding [quality of this] disorder is the children's inability to relate themselves in the ordinary way to people and situations. . . . Profound aloneness dominates all behavior."
- The child with autism "has good relation to objects; he is interested in them, can play with them happily for hours . . . the child's relation to people is altogether different."
- "The child's noises and motions and all his performances are as monotonously repetitious as are his verbal utterances. . . . The child's behavior is governed by an anxiously obsessive desire for the maintenance of sameness."

Research Project

To understand autism better, read other fiction about this topic. Write a report on each book. A different book will be listed in each chapter. If you can't find these books in your library, ask your librarian to order them for you or help you find other books to replace them. Here's the first on your list:

Anything but Typical by Nora Raleigh Baskin

Some children with autism have an amazing ability to remember complex patterns and sequences, which can allow them to perform music skillfully.

Make Connections: What's In A Word?

The word "autistic" comes from the Greek word "autos," which means self. The term describes conditions in which a person is removed from social interaction—an isolated self.

- "The astounding vocabulary of the speaking children, the excellent memory for events of several years before, the phenomenal rote memory for poems and names, and the precise recollection of complex patterns and sequences, bespeak good intelligence."

When autism was first studied, many professionals believed that it was the result of a "cold" and uncaring mother. However, current research has dispelled that notion. Says Uta Frith, author of several books on autism, children with autism "are not made autistic by parents who did not love them enough. Autism . . . can hit anyone, any family, without warning. Its biological origin is likely to be well before birth."

Text-Dependent Questions

1. When does autism begin?
2. Explain what a spectrum disorder is.
3. What is the M-CHAT? Why is it used?
4. When was autism first described?
5. What does the word "autism" mean and why is it appropriate for people with this condition?

*Some questions take all our courage to ask.
Living the answers may take all our strength.*
—Carl Lewis

Words to Understand

infant intervention professional: A person who has knowledge of developmental patterns typical of infants and toddlers and then uses that knowledge to assess a particular infant's level of development.

language skills: Using and understanding language.

adaptive progress: Adjusting to environmental conditions at a pace consistent with others of the same age.

neurologist: A physician skilled in the diagnosis and treatment of diseases of the nervous system.

EEG: The recording and tracing of brain waves.

prognosis: The prospect of recovery as is normally seen in the course of a disease.

2

THE SEARCH BEGINS

Meeting with the audiologist was scary for Tucker. He hated to travel and it was a long drive. The office was very bright, music played, and Mom and Dad had to answer quite a few questions. Tucker sat on Mom's lap, and he kept putting his hands to his ears.

"He certainly seemed to be able to hear well, almost too well. It was as if everything was too loud for him," Dad said at dinner that night.

A week later, they learned Dad was right, Tucker's hearing results were normal. Mom's other investigations into what might be Tucker's problem had led her to a program offered from state to state called Birth to Three. After speaking to a counselor there a few times, she arranged for an ***infant intervention professional*** to come to the house to evaluate Tucker.

"The evaluator, told me she wanted to check Tucker's ***language skills***," Mom said that evening. "But while she was here she also observed his physical, social, and ***adaptive progress***." Livie didn't understand what all those words meant, and she felt worried.

"Wow, quite a lot to address in one morning. How was he?" Dad asked.

Mom sighed. "Well, I guess he was typically Tucker. While she asked questions, he sat in his corner with his car—actually both cars. First, setting one up on the table, knocking it off, and then setting the other on the table and knocking it off. One after the other, right in order every time."

"What did she say about that?"

Mom stirred the gravy. "She said he had some developmental delays. Sometimes that is a problem and sometimes it works itself out."

Dad set the table. "Another person who sees something wrong, but what? When will we hear back from her?"

"Sometime in the next two weeks. The doctor returned my call today. He suggested we also see a **neurologist**. I called for an appointment, but we can't get in until six weeks from now. I think I'll ask the infant intervention evaluator if she can help us get an earlier appointment. Her name's Margie, and I like her. She seemed to understand Tucker."

"Mom, my birthday is in seven weeks," Livie said. "I counted it on the calendar today."

Dad was frowning. "I'd like to get to the bottom of this as soon as possible."

"Am I going to have a party this year?" Livie looked from Mom to Dad. Mom looked tired. Mom and Dad kept talking about Tucker. No one said anything about Livie's birthday.

Livie's mother began to read every book she could find on developmental problems in younger children. She soon learned about autism, and the more she read the more she wondered if Tucker had this disorder.

One day she mentioned some of her findings to Livie's father. "It says that children with autism have three major areas of impairment: social skills, language skills, and activity or behavioral skills. Nate, this scares me. I think this sounds a lot like Tucker."

Dad was frowning. He seemed to do that a lot lately. "Has anyone else who's seen Tucker mentioned autism?"

"No, but it is a developmental disorder and Margie said—"

"Let's just see what Margie or the Birth to Three offices or whoever says after they look at the evaluation," Dad interrupted. "There's no sense in worrying about something that is probably not true."

When Livie's parents met with Margie at her office, she recommended that Tucker see a neurologist who would be able to administer the necessary testing to help understand Tucker's development problems more clearly.

Livie's parents and Tucker left for the appointment early one school morning. They had to drive about an hour and a half, and they left before Livie's bus arrived, so Grandma Montgomery came to help her get breakfast and meet the bus. Livie worried about Tucker all day.

Later that day her parents explained to Grandma and Grandpa what had happened. Livie listened from the family room where Tucker sat in the corner with a cup he had gotten at McDonald's that day. It was Tucker's first of many cups and many more appointments.

"The doctor asked us every question you can imagine—from what Tucker did first thing in the morning, to how and what he ate, to whether or not he watched TV. It took almost two hours," Dad was saying.

"Tucker was so good," Mom said.

Livie heard her father sigh. "Yes, he was great, most of the time, because we didn't bother him, and he had that cup."

No one said anything else and plans were made for three weeks from then when Tucker needed to have more tests.

Grandma came to stay with Livie again, while her parents and Tucker took another trip to the city. They were tired when they returned.

"The tests were hard on him," Mom said. "But he was a good little trooper."

"Except when he had to go for the blood tests and the **_EEG_**, then he got upset. And when anyone touched his Burger King cup, he tried to bite them." Dad sounded angry.

Livie left the room to get a drink. Her father's tone scared her.

When she came back, her mother was holding her head in her hands. "Nate, why are you talking like this? Things are bad enough without you making them worse."

"What do you mean, why am I talking like this?" Dad's voice got louder, and Livie wished she had stayed in the kitchen. "We have to take our son for all these tests. And I see how everyone looks at him. Some look like they feel sorry and others look like they think he's an interesting curiosity. And after all that, we still don't know what's wrong with him." He sighed. "I guess I'm tired. Maybe I need some fresh air." He walked out and slammed the door behind him.

With Dad acting so angry, Mom began calling Margie whenever she had questions about Tucker. She told Margie she had been reading about autism and she was afraid that was what was wrong with Tucker. Margie did not want to commit to any diagnosis, but she answered Mom's questions. If Margie didn't know the answers, she helped Mom find them.

Margie told her that the appointment with the neurologist sounded like it was pretty routine. Although no test could prove a child had developmental problems like autism, some tests definitely ruled out other medical problems.

Livie would sit quietly listening while her mother talked to Margie on the phone. She was trying to piece together in her own mind what was going on with her brother, but she didn't understand a lot of the words her mother was using. When Mom hung up one day, Livie asked, "What's early intervention?"

"If the doctors find out that Tucker has autism, early intervention means they want to start treating him as soon as possible."

"Will he have to take medicine to get better?"

"I don't think so, Livie. There is no medicine to make someone with autism get better."

Mom looked so sad that Livie started to cry. "Will he have to go into the hospital? Will he die?"

Her mother put her arm around her. "No, Livie, he's not going to die. And we don't know for sure if he even has autism. The doctors just don't know until they are finished with the testing. Maybe he's just going through a stage and he'll get better by himself."

The next appointment with the neurologist was another long day. Mom and Dad found out the answer to the question everyone kept asking but no one really wanted to hear. Did Tucker have autism? The answer was yes.

Mom sat with a cup of tea. Dad paced around the room picking up dishes, toys, and stacking mail. Grandma and Grandpa sat quietly.

"Go ahead, tell them," Mom said. "We have to learn to say it, Nate."

Livie's father gave an angry shrug. "You mean tell them it's worse than we expected? Tell them our son has autism and the doctor can't even tell us what will happen next, let alone what will happen in a year or two years or five years?" Dad gripped the edge of the kitchen counter until his knuckles turned white. "Now we have to go to a developmental specialist. Maybe she'll give us the ***prognosis*** or maybe we'll have to go somewhere else after that. We don't even have a life anymore."

Mom began to cry, and Livie felt sick to her stomach. Grandma put her arms around Mom, and Grandpa hugged Dad. Then without another word, the adults set the table and finished preparing the meal. Livie could hardly eat a thing.

"I think we need to find out as much information as we can so we know what to expect and understand what is going on," Mom said.

Tucker sat in his high chair eating mashed potatoes and holding his cup, the newest one he had gotten today at Burger King. He turned it around and around and then hit himself in the teeth with it. No one said a thing.

Make Connections: Autistic Speech

Persons with autism who are able to communicate through speech are sometimes thought to be "preachy" when they speak. Their subjects are often monologues about something particularly important to them. They lack the ability to understand another person's point of view and do not consider conversation a two-way interaction.

BIRTH TO THREE

Intervention in developmental issues for babies and toddlers represents much of the work done in the state-to-state programs of Birth to Three. Each state or even locality of Birth to Three works with families to help ensure that their child is moving step by step along the developmental scale. Any deviations in language, social, or behavioral patterns are tested

Occasionally, a child with autism may be able to relate to a pet, even though he has difficulty interacting with family members.

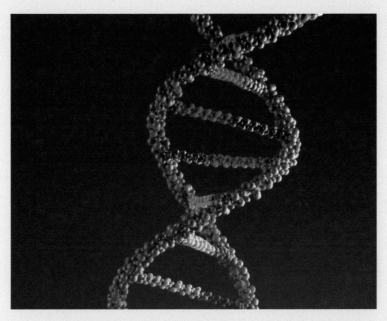

A strand of DNA may hold the secret to autism's cause.

and monitored with the knowledge that early intervention
on developmental issues makes a great difference in the life
of a child.

WHAT CAUSES AUTISM?

Brain scans of people with autism show differences in the
shape and structure of the brain that may account for the
problems in understanding sensory input. Genetic studies
point to the incidence of autism in identical twins and
within generations of families as an indicator that there is a
genetic factor to be considered in the disorder. Researchers
have not yet found a particular gene that causes autism. But
they continue to see evidence that there might be answers

within the genetic code. Another possibility is that a cluster of unstable genes may cause a problem while the brain is developing. This interference may lead to autism.

Problems during pregnancy or even delivery are being studied, as well as environmental factors such as viral infections or exposure to chemicals. The answers to these questions could change the outlook of the disorder in the future.

DIAGNOSING AUTISM

Because there are no medical tests that confirm a diagnosis of autism, children must be evaluated by questioning parents or caretakers, observation of behavior, and consideration of developmental levels. Usually a hearing and speech specialist will be involved in these evaluations as well as a neurologist and possibly a developmental specialist.

Several screening tests are used to identify persons with autism.

CARS Rating Scale
(Childhood Autism Rating Scale)

This screening device was developed by Eric Schopler in the early 1970s. It uses observation of behavior to evaluate the person using a 15-point scale. Some skills targeted in the assessment are: relationships with other people, whether the child makes eye contact, level of coordination, and the level of the child's listening response.

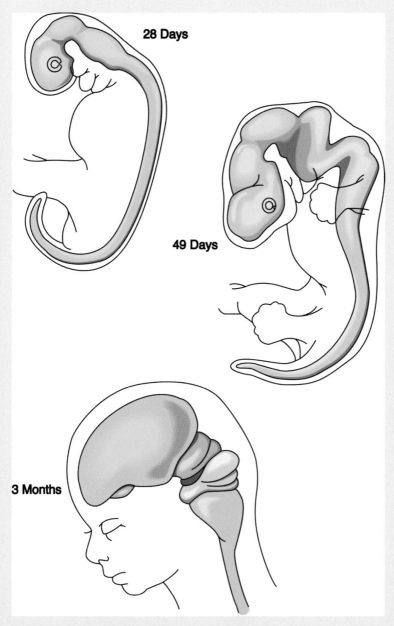

Autism may be caused by some problem in the developing brain of an embryo.

Make Connections: Is Autism Increasing?

 Today as many as one in every 88 children is diagnosed as being somewhere on the autistism spectrum, when as few as twenty-five years ago only one in every 10,000 were identified. Some of this increase may be due to the fact that educators, families, and medical professionals are more sensitive to autism spectrum symptoms than they used to be. In the past, someone might have been considered "odd" or "eccentric" without being labeled as autistic. However, researchers can't rule out that there is actually a rise in autism taking place—but if so, they don't know why.

The Modified Checklist for Autism in Toddlers (M-CHAT)

This checklist (described in chapter 1) was developed by Diana Robins, Deborah Fein, and Marianne Barton in 1999. This tool can be used on a child as young as sixteen months. A questionnaire completed by the parents, and a follow-up with a healthcare provider, supply information used in making an evaluation. This screening consists of fourteen questions, and it is used to evaluate babies between the ages of fourteen and fifteen months.

MIND THEORIES

Most persons with autism do not understand what other people are feeling or believing about a particular situation. In other words, they react to the situation just as it is acted out, not taking into consideration that the other person

A child with autism is often fascinated by spinning objects.

Research Project

Al Capone Does My Shirts by Gennifer Choldenko

This Newbery Honor book tells the story of a brother and his older sister who has autism. It also gives a glimpse into the infamous Alcatraz Prison.

might have plans, thoughts, or even points of view that might alter what can be seen right at the moment. They can't put themselves in "someone else's shoes."

This may be the reason autistic children have difficulty making friends, communicating, and having other social interactions. For example, an autistic child does not understand that he may upset a friend if he suddenly gets up and leaves.

MAKING OTHERS AWARE OF AUTISM

On November 21, 2002, Congressman Dan Burton, Chairman of the Committee on Government Reform wrote to President Bush urging him to host a White House conference on autism. He pointed to a recent study funded by the State of California citing the increasing incidence of autism in California. The information showed that three times as many children were diagnosed with autism over the past ten years than previously.

Congressman Burton called for solutions to help families cope with the emotional and financial care for their children. Prior to this, Congressman Burton had been instrumental in calling for a stop to the use of the mercury-based product

Text-Dependent Questions

1. Why is speech so difficult for a child with autism?
2. What are some of the possible causes of autism?
3. Explain why Dan Burton is an important figure in the world of autism.

Thimerosal in vaccines for young children. Some professionals, as well as parents, believe the amount of mercury used in vaccines may be responsible for children becoming autistic, although there is no scientific research to support this.

Congressman Burton also helped make possible the opening of the Christian Sarkine Autism Treatment Center. Named after Burton's grandson, who is being treated for autism, the center has done research sponsored by the National Institute of Mental Health, the Centers for Disease Control, and the Department of Education.

On the floor of the U.S. House of Representatives, Burton has also read letters and showed pictures from families with autistic children in an effort to raise public awareness of the autism epidemic. Burton retired from Congress in 2012.

Some problems are too big for just one person. But together, even the smallest people can do great things.
—Gary Russell

Words to Understand

Applied Behavior Analysis (ABA): An educational approach to the treatment of autism that includes rewarding good behavior in order to make it more desirable than unwanted behavior.

early intervention: Beginning a program of education at the earliest time in the autistic child's life, preferably when the child is less than five years of age.

intense learning: An extreme degree of learning marked by or expressive of great zeal, energy, determination, and concentration.

acclimated: Adapted to a new environment or situation.

desensitize: To help a person get used to an upsetting or painful stimulation.

3

Looking for Help

Livie's relatives came to dinner that Friday night. After more crying and hugging and a few strolls around the neighborhood, the adults began to talk about what to do first. Mom got out all her notes, things she had read, and things Margie had told her about the available resources at Birth to Three. After dinner, Livie and her cousins went to watch a video they had brought. But Livie really wanted to stay and listen to the adults. Everyone was very serious. Books, pamphlets, notes, and printed papers from the Internet were spread out on the dining-room table.

Livie's parents were trying to decide how to care for Tucker. The adults talked for hours about what to do next.

"The specialist said that the sooner we begin some kind of education or therapy, the better it will be for Tucker." Livie was glad her father no longer sounded so angry.

"I read that too, Nate. And I read about a kind of behavioral therapy a Doctor Lovaas from California has been using," Mom added.

Dad sighed. "Everything you read says you can't always know the extent of the disability until the child is older. Since Tucker is only two and a half, we don't know what will happen in his case."

Mom began to cry again. "I'm scared. I know you'll all help, but I still can't believe this is happening. I keep hoping it's not true."

"One of the problems is knowing our choices," Dad said. "We don't know what's available at our school district, and Tucker isn't old enough to participate in any of those programs anyway. That's where Birth to Three comes in—but we will just get him started there and he'll turn three, which is when their services end. We're right at this in-between place."

"It's so confusing." Mom leaned on the table. "Look at all these notes. It takes a lot of work and time to investigate."

Dad looked around the table at their family. "If you help us, maybe we can figure out something. At least it will be a start. If Tucker is only in one program for a few months, so what? If the doctor says doing something quickly makes a difference, then that's what we have to do. I wonder if there are any local autistic programs or even any support groups."

Mom looked down at her hands. "What if we make the wrong choice?"

Livie decided it was time to remind her parents that Tucker wasn't the only thing in the world. "Mom, did we decide on my birthday yet?"

Her mother looked up and smiled. "Dad and I think we should have your party when the weather gets a little nicer. Wouldn't you like a summer party this year? It could be a pool party."

Livie didn't say anything. No party for her real birthday sounded bad. But she loved to swim.

"Let's not decide now," Dad said. "We'll talk about it tomorrow."

Over the next few weeks Livie heard words like **Applied Behavior Analysis** (ABA), **early intervention**, and **intense learning**. They all had to do with Tucker. Tucker—the reason she had only cake and ice cream with her family and no party on her birthday. Tucker—the reason they weren't going to the beach this year. Tucker—crying, screaming Tucker. Livie hoped her parents would remember her pool party this summer. But she wasn't too sure they would.

One day when she came home from school, Livie heard her mother talking on the phone to Grandma again. Livie listened as Mom explained ABA. She said that ABA stands for Applied Behavior Analysis, and it's a way to teach autistic children, like how Mrs. Spencer taught Livie in school. Only this way of teaching was done mostly with one student and one teacher. Tucker would be the only student in his class because he needed to be able to really concentrate on what his teacher was telling him, so he had to be right with her all the time. And the teacher needed to show everyone else how to work with Tucker, too.

"All of us get to help teach him," Mom said to Grandma.

Livie thought that sounded like fun; she'd like to tell Tucker what to do. Maybe she could teach him to act normal. But he cried so much, she wasn't sure how she could get him to listen to her. It didn't seem like he wanted to be good.

That night Mom and Dad talked about the different teaching ideas for Tucker. They included Livie whenever they could.

"Some people believe an autistic child needs about forty hours of instruction each week. I made some more phone calls but there's no one around here doing any of this kind of work with autistic kids." Mom looked tired and discouraged.

Dad was reading some papers, looking thoughtful. "Whoever teaches Tucker would try to replace any of his undesirable behaviors with more acceptable conduct by working with him over and over. Repeat the one concept for long periods of time each day. Eight hours a day. That sounds like a lot of time for him. He's not even three years old yet."

"That's how it's supposed to work. Everything is in small pieces. Some work, some play, with us reinforcing everything during the rest of the day. He might start with learning to look at people instead of looking right past us or through us. There's lots of reinforcement, which includes favorite things like foods, fun toys, and anything else that might get his attention. Not everyone thinks you have to work such long hours or that the reinforcement should be given in things like treats, but definitely intensive therapy is the thing most professionals believe works best." Mom's voice sounded a little more hopeful.

"I'm going to learn to help Tucker, too," Livie said.

"That's great, Livie. We can certainly use all the help we can get."

"When he turns three," Mom added, "there's the special pre-school at the elementary school he can attend. I think they go from nine until eleven thirty. And I guess we could continue to look for a therapist who could come here during the afternoon."

"He's going to go to my school?" Livie asked. "Will he scream and cry like he does here?"

Mom and Dad looked at each other. "He would have his own bus, and the classroom is away from the regular classes. But let's not think about that yet. We haven't decided what we want to do, so there's no sense in wondering what will happen."

Livie was glad Tucker would at least ride his own bus. But she thought it might be embarrassing to hear her brother screaming at school.

Mom interrupted Livie's thoughts "Until he turns three, I guess we should put him in the Birth to Three program for developmentally delayed children. He would go to a class two mornings a week and once a week the teacher would visit him here. Of course, like the elementary school program, there will be other children in the class with different problems, so we just have to see how it would work for Tucker."

"I guess for now that's what we'll do—but let's keep looking for a behavioral therapist who could work with him and teach us how to help him too." Dad got up to answer the phone and the discussion ended.

Tucker began going to "school" on Tuesday and Thursday mornings. He was not happy there. After three weeks, Mom and Margie discussed what they should do next.

"He's been more unhappy at home too. He's even giving us problems at bedtime, much worse than ever before. And I'm sure the lack of sleep isn't helping any of us."

"It's only been six weeks," Margie told Mom. "It often takes children, especially those with autism, some time to get ***acclimated***. But I'm concerned that Tucker doesn't seem to be getting better or even acting the same. His behavior gets worse each week."

"Is there anything we can do to get through this?" Mom asked.

"I've asked for a one-on-one assistant next week," Margie said. "She'll spend all her time with Tucker, so maybe she or I will be able to figure out something."

Livie had been so excited when Tucker started school, but now everything seemed wrong. She had hoped the teachers would show Tucker how to act like other kids. Tucker wasn't supposed to get worse.

Every night Mom and Dad took turns trying to keep Tucker in bed. He cried and cried. Livie wondered if she would ever again go to sleep without hearing the sound of his crying and her parents' voices trying to soothe him. She lay in bed, wishing Mom and Dad were talking to her every night, trying to read or singing or whatever. She wished Tucker could understand how much they were trying to help him. She wished she wasn't all alone in her bedroom.

FAMILIES WHO COPE WITH AUTISM

When one member of a family has autism, the entire family is faced with emotional tension. Some family members may feel angry, others may feel sad and depressed, and others may want to deny that the problem even exists. Every member of the family will probably experience some of these feelings at times.

Parents of a child who has autism will find new stress placed on their marriage. And siblings will also need help coping with their feelings.

Dr. Derenda Timmons Schubert, of Pacific Northwest Children's Services in Portland, Oregon, recommends that parents be aware of how children at various ages will cope differently with a sibling who has autism.

Preschoolers

Children in this age group can't usually put their feelings into words, so they will likely show their feelings through behaviors. They will be unable to understand the special needs of their sibling, but they will notice differences and try to teach their brother or sister. Children of this age may be more likely to enjoy their sibling because they have not yet learned to be judgmental.

Elementary School Age

Since these children go out into the school world, they are much more aware of the differences between people. They have the ability to understand a definition and explanation of their sibling's special need as long as it is explained to them in terms they can understand. They may worry that the disability is contagious or wonder if something is wrong with them, too. They may also experience guilt for having

Children with autism may respond to one-on-one instruction.

negative thoughts or feelings about their sibling. Children of this age may become over-helpful and well-behaved—or they may misbehave to get their parents' attention. School-age children often have conflicting feelings about their sibling. But this is true as well in sibling relationships that do not include a disability.

Adolescents

Adolescents have the capability of understanding more elaborate explanations of autism. They may ask detailed questions. Adolescence is the time when individuals begin discovering who they are outside the family, while at the same time, fitting in with a peer group is important. As a result, children this age may be embarrassed by their sibling in front of friends and dates. They may feel torn between their desire for independence from the family and wanting to maintain a special relationship with their sibling. They may resent the amount of responsibility they have for their sibling, and they may begin worrying about their sibling's future.

Professional support and counseling can help families better cope with a member who has autism.

HOW THE AUTISM SPECTRUM CHANGED

In 2013, the American Psychiatric Association's Diagnostic and Statistical Manual of Mental Disorders, fifth edition (DSM-5), removed many of the familiar autism spectrum diagnoses that were found in the fourth edition (DSM-IV). The reasoning behind these eliminations was that there was no consistency with which the removed disorders were applied.

Those that were removed include:

Appropriate eating behaviors may be a struggle even for individuals with autism.

- **Asperger's Syndrome** in which individuals function at a higher level with more subtle displays of impairment in social and language skills.
- **Childhood Disintegrative Disorder (CDD),** which is the regressive form of pervasive developmental disorder (PDD) where the child seems to develop normally for the first two years but then begins to lose skills in at least two major areas including language, play, social skills, bowel or bladder control, or motor skills.

WHAT IS IT LIKE TO HAVE AUTISM?

As a child, Temple Grandin was very sensitive to touch. Sometimes her clothes hurt when they contacted her skin. Even people hugging her made her cringe and pull away. This is one of the problems associated with autism. But fortunately for Temple, her parents began early intervention when she was only two and a half years old, which she believes helped her to handle her autism. She was able to attend grade school, and in a private school she met a science teacher who nurtured her interest in animal science. She entered college and continued her schooling. Today she is Dr. Temple Grandin, Professor of Animal Science at Colorado State University.

Grandin has designed equipment to help in the use of handling cattle and other animals. Her book *Emergence: Labeled Autistic* has introduced many to what it is like to live with problems of touch, speech, and social understanding. For her, the world as normal persons know it is difficult to understand. Her book *Thinking in Pictures* is also about autism.

When she was only eighteen, Grandin invented a squeeze machine. She thought of making the machine after visiting her aunt's ranch. There she noticed that the cattle

Research Project

Temple Grandin: How the Girl Who Loved Cows Embraced Autism and Changed the World by Sy Montgomery and Temple Grandin

Coauthored by Temple Grandin herself, this biography will give you a broader view of autism, while also telling you the story of a fascinating individual.

being herded through a squeeze chute seemed to calm down once they began to feel the pressure that was applied. Grandin tried the chute herself and felt relieved for a few hours afterward. The apparatus she created was completely lined with foam rubber and could be operated by the person inside the machine. Having control over the amount and duration of the pressure allowed Grandin to **desensitize** her delicate feelings of touch. Grandin feels that by allowing the machine to teach her about the comfort of touch she is able to share that comfort of touch with others.

Unlike many individuals with autism who are less high-functioning, Grandin was able to communicate as she grew older. As a child, she says she knew that parents and teachers could not understand why she could only scream when she wanted to communicate, but at the time she had no other way to communicate. It was the only way she knew to reach the outside world.

To this day Grandin has a problem with certain smooth, coordinated movements. She tells of being able to operate hydraulic equipment that has a series of levers, but says she can only use one lever at a time. Coordinating two levers at once is impossible for her.

Finding the right way to teach students with autism is key. What works for one student may not work for another.

Text-Dependent Questions

1. What are some ways that children and young adults will react differently at different ages to a sibling with autism?
2. Who is Temple Grandin?

Grandin explains that she hears things as if she is wearing a hearing aid with the volume turned all the way up. Grandin has a problem screening out certain noises and then trying to key in on others. She learned to tune out sound when she was very young. Because of this, her mother thought Grandin was deaf.

Just like the young children who tune others out or separate themselves, Grandin feels that she still needs to work to overcome the sensory problems of autism.

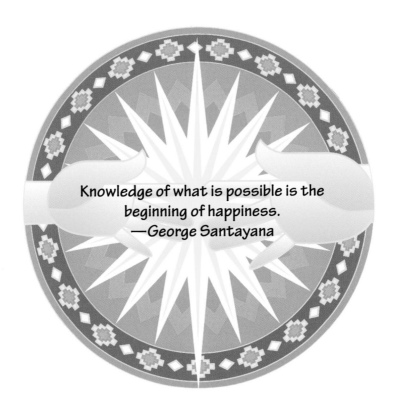

Knowledge of what is possible is the
beginning of happiness.
—George Santayana

Words to Understand

Individualized Education Plan (IEP): A special education program designed to meet the individual needs of a child.

due process: Legal, formal procedures that protect a person from arbitrary, illegal, or unfair action on the part of law enforcement officers.

elicit: To bring forth, trigger, or cause.

4

CHOOSING THE RIGHT ROUTE

Livie's mother didn't have a party for Tucker's third birthday. Instead, she had a dinner. She couldn't bear to think of little children running all around chasing each other when her son would be sitting in the corner with a cup. She wanted Tucker to be the happy little boy she had hoped to have, opening presents and eating birthday cake and ice cream.

Tucker didn't even like ice cream. It made him gag, like most cold things he tried to eat. Mom still warmed his milk in the microwave before he would drink it.

So all the adults in Livie's family sat around the table at Tucker's birthday dinner, while Livie's cousins escaped as soon as they could to play in the yard. Livie lingered for a while, hoping that one of her aunts or uncles would offer to organize a game for the kids. But no one did. Everyone just sat quietly sipping their after-dinner coffee.

Livie missed going to her aunts and uncles' houses. Now everyone always came to her parents' house for family gatherings. Livie's family never even went to Grandma's house anymore, because the last time they went to Grandma's for dinner, Tucker screamed the whole time they were there. Everyone just watched Mom and Dad trying to get Tucker to settle down, and no one enjoyed Grandma's dinner. When they finally started home that night, Tucker fell asleep in the car, only to wake up when Dad took him out of his car seat; then he started screaming all over again.

57

When Mom got Tucker ready for bed that night, Livie looked up at her father and said, "Why does Tucker ruin everything?"

Her father sighed. "Tucker doesn't like anything to change. He can't handle going to Grandma's house, because everything is different there from what he is used to."

But Livie didn't want to think of Tucker now. She just wanted to enjoy Grandma's special chocolate cake, and then she wanted to go outside and play with her cousins.

Livie loved having her cousins over. They played with her like real kids, and she wasn't so lonely when they were around. Her aunt had suggested that Livie spend the next weekend with her cousins, and Livie was thrilled.

After dessert, the adults began "Tucker talk."

"I just don't know if I want to send him back to school, again," Mom said.

Livie's father shook his head. "Everyone keeps telling us that he needs as much learning structure as possible. It's all a part of the early intervention. We're lucky in a way, you know. I read about a woman who went from doctor to doctor and no one understood what was wrong with her daughter. Finally, when the girl was ten years old someone diagnosed her with autism. I felt bad when I read that. Can you imagine how that mother must feel? When the child begins therapy at a younger age, there seems to be a greater recovery to some normal behaviors and learning patterns."

"You see how he is," her mother said to Livie's aunt. "I think he's getting worse. When Livie went to give him a present, she told him she'd hold his cup so he could look at his new toy. He bit her."

"Yeah, and it hurt." Livie looked down at her hand. "Mom had to use three Band-Aids."

"Does he always ride that thing for so long?" Grandpa asked, pointing to the corner where Tucker was going back and forth on a rocking horse. "He's been doing that for nearly an hour."

Livie's father shook his head. "An hour is not that long. Once he rode that thing for two hours and twenty minutes. Just back and forth, not one sound and never a glance at his mother, Livie, or me," Dad said.

"I wish we could find someone to come here. But maybe the program at the public school will help." Mom looked like she might cry, and she looked scared too—and tired. Livie's stomach hurt.

Two weeks later, Mom and Dad met with Tucker's new teacher, the school principal, and the school psychologist. Because Tucker was now enrolled in the special preschool in the local school district, an **Individualized Education Plan (IEP)** needed to be written. This included the goals Mom and Dad and his teacher hoped Tucker would accomplish for the coming year. Mom and Dad's input was crucial because they knew Tucker best, and they were needed to help carry through what was decided at the meeting. Of course, this meant still more meetings, as the school and the family monitored Tucker's progress. Livie sometimes thought that "Tucker meetings" were about the only thing her parents did anymore.

The same day that Livie's parents had their meeting at school, Livie burst into the kitchen after she got off the bus. "Our principal talked to me in the lunch line today."

"Well, aren't you the special girl." Dad picked up Livie and twirled her around.

"He told me he met you and Mom."

Mom nodded. "After we talked about Tucker, your principal told us about some problems you're having in school."

Livie bit her lip. "I'm fine," she said quickly, but she felt that pain in her stomach again.

"He said your teacher had asked him if he knew of any problems at home because you're not answering in class. Your teacher doesn't think you're feeling well either. She said you've gone to the nurse a few times lately. What's wrong?"

"It's just those stomachaches. I probably eat too fast."

"Try to slow down when eating. And how about talking a little more in class?" Dad asked.

"Okay." Livie walked to her room. She hated feeling sick all the time, but she wouldn't go the nurse anymore, no matter what.

Tucker started school the next week. Mrs. Anderson, his new teacher, had some experience with teaching autistic children and she wasn't surprised that Tucker spent the first week and a half lying on the floor, much of the time throwing a tantrum. She tried to reassure Mom this was normal and he would be fine.

When Mom picked Tucker up one day during his second week of school, Mrs. Anderson introduced her to Anita Fuller. Her son Carl was in Tucker's class.

"I was wondering if you and Tucker would want to come to our house for lunch tomorrow," Anita asked Livie's mother. "Don't worry," Anita added quickly, "I help out in class occasionally and I've spent some time with Tucker. Besides, there's nothing I haven't seen. Carl is autistic, too. He's six and has been in the program for a little over two years. I just thought we could talk and share some experiences."

Livie's mother hadn't met anyone yet who had an autistic child too. The next day she and Tucker went to lunch at their new friends' house. At dinner that night Dad and Livie were eager to hear what happened.

"Well, of course, I brought all Tucker's cups, hoping he would be happy with at least one of them. Anita is wonderful. She asked what he liked to eat, what he did when he was content, and she told me lots of things about Carl and their struggle to get help." Mom took a bite of her salad and looked thoughtful. "Even though Tucker screamed the way he always does someplace unfamiliar, Anita assured me it didn't bother her. And she meant it; she knows just how I feel. We got out Carl's rocking horse, which he never rides—he just turns it over and tries to line up cars on the rockers. Tucker sat there for awhile screaming, but soon he started rocking and for a while he was quiet."

"Did Carl and Tucker play?" Livie asked.

"No, but Carl did look at Tucker once. At least I thought he did. I hate to say it, but I think they have a harder time with Carl than we do with Tucker. Carl still wears diapers, which he often takes off and throws around, even after they are soiled. He also has run away four times. The whole house has a security system from the inside, so he can't slip away. The last time he disappeared, he somehow got to a neighborhood pond and went in. He loves water."

"I'm glad we don't have any of that to deal with," Dad said. "I guess we're lucky." He sounded almost amazed to hear himself saying the words.

"Does Carl know how to swim?" Livie wanted to know.

"Well, they take him swimming a lot. But no, they don't feel he can swim well enough to save himself. Fortunately, a neighbor saw him and helped him out, which wasn't easy because he also bites and kicks. He's a pretty big boy, twice the size of Tucker. And by that time he was scared and he didn't know the guy well. I felt so bad when Anita was telling me about it."

"Mom, we'll keep our doors locked all the time from now on," Livie said. She didn't like the idea of Tucker wandering around by himself.

"Thanks, Livie." Her mother smiled at her. "Anita told me she heard that the college about forty miles north of here teaches special education. She suggested I look there for someone to teach Tucker."

"Do Carl's parents do more than send him to special preschool?" Dad asked.

"Yes, they have a speech therapist, who is employed by the school district, one afternoon a week. The therapist helps Carl learn to say words, but she also wants him to understand what he's saying, not to just repeat what he hears. He does say a few words now. Carl talked a little when he was a toddler, but he was nonverbal until about the last month or so. Now he says 'da da,' 'bye,' and 'one, two, three.' Oh, and he loves light switches. He constantly turns them on and off."

Livie's stomach began to hurt again. She wondered if Tucker would keep getting worse instead of getting better.

THE RIGHT TO LEARN

Since 1973, a series of federal and state laws and court decisions have supported the rights of individuals with disabilities to fully participate in all aspects of our society. Section 504 of the Rehabilitation Act of 1973, a civil rights law, prohibits the discrimination of individuals with disabilities, and provides *due process* where discrimination might have occurred. The Americans with Disabilities Act, signed by President George H. W. Bush in 1992, reinforced Section 504; this later act called for the "full inclusion" of individuals with disabilities in all aspects of our society, including transportation, telecommunications, and education.

In 1975, the 94th Congress passed the landmark Education for the Handicapped Act, known as Public Law 94-142. Reauthorized in 2004 as the Individuals with Disabilities Education Act (IDEA), this law provides states with federal monies to serve the needs of individuals with disabilities, ages three to twenty-one.

This is achieved through a very specific process defined within that law. *All* preschool and school-age students, regardless of the severity of their disability, must be provided an "appropriate education" in the "least restrictive environment." A multi-disciplinary team, which includes the parent, conducts an evaluation that identifies a student's eligibility and needs, and uses an individualized education plan (IEP) to describe a program that meets that student's needs. To ensure that the educational program is appropriate to the child's current (and evolving) needs, programs must be reviewed at least annually, with periodic re-evaluations conducted at least every three years.

Before these laws, children with disabilities like autism were not guaranteed the right to an appropriate education. Institutionalization was more common, and as adults, they were often excluded from the rest of our society. Society was

A special education teacher works with a classroom of children with autism. These students may also have other impairments.

apt to view individuals with disabilities with suspicion, con-
demning them (or their parents) for their problems. Scientific
research has helped us better understand the reality and
potential of people with disabilities like autism.

INDIVIDUALIZED EDUCATION PLAN (IEP)

An IEP is a written plan designed specifically for each child
who qualifies for special education. It defines reasonable ex-
pectations for achievement and how success will be deter-
mined. According to the U.S. Department of Education, it
should include these points:

1. Current performance. The IEP must state how the
   child is currently doing in school (known as present
   levels of educational performance).
2. Annual goals. These are goals that the child can
   reasonably accomplish in a year. The goals are broken
   down into short-term objectives or benchmarks.
3. Special education and related services. The IEP must
   list the special education and related services to be
   provided to the child or on behalf of the child.
4. Participation with nondisabled children. The IEP must
   explain the extent (if any) to which the child will not
   participate with nondisabled children in the regular
   class and other school activities.
5. Participation in state and district-wide tests. Most
   states and districts give achievement tests to children
   in certain grades or age groups. The IEP must state
   what modifications in the administration of these tests
   the child will need. If a test is not appropriate for the
   child, the IEP must state why the test is not
   appropriate and how the child will be tested instead.
6. Dates and places. The IEP must state when services
   will begin, how often they will be provided, where
   they will be provided, and how long they will last.

Students with autism benefit from physical exercise.

7. Transition service needs. Beginning when the child is age 14 (or younger, if appropriate), the IEP must address (within the applicable parts of the IEP) the courses he or she needs to take to reach his or her post-school goals.
8. Needed transition services. Beginning when the child is age 16 (or younger, if appropriate), the IEP must state what transition services are needed to help the child prepare for leaving school.
9. Age of majority. Beginning at least one year before the child reaches the age of majority, the IEP must include a statement that the student has been told of any rights that will transfer to him or her at the age of majority.
10. Measuring progress. The IEP must state how the child's progress will be measured and how parents will be informed of that progress.

TREATMENT FOR AUTISM

Early Intervention

Studies show that early intervention makes a great difference in the lives of children diagnosed with autism. Highly structured educational programs designed to fit the needs of the individual child provide the most productive atmosphere. The intensity of the program seems to make a difference also. A particular plan needs to be more of a way of life rather than just a teaching session.

Such intervention might include communication therapy, social skill development, sensory integration therapy, and applied behavioral analysis. One-on-one teaching may be needed according to the severity of the challenges.

An emphasis on living skills may also be included in these programs. Like all children, autistic children need to learn safety strategies, such as how to cross the street, how to behave around fires and hot stoves, how to maneuver up and down stairs, and other behaviors needed to move toward independence. Several specific programs have been developed to address the treatment needs of children with autism.

Applied Behavior Analysis (ABA)

Although there is some controversy about the intensity of behavioral teaching needed to help autistic children become more responsive to the world around them, most authorities

Early intervention is important for children with autism.

agree that at least some training in this area makes a difference in level of functioning.

Initiated in 1968 by Dr. Ivor Lovaas, ABA is based on rewarding desired behavior. Appropriate behavior is repeated again and again until it becomes a part of the child's understanding.

One of the premises of this training is that it be designed for the specific child in question. The therapist begins by questioning the parents and observing the child. While observing behavior, the therapist or parent recognizes everything that precedes the behavior—where the child was, what she was doing at the time, and whether she was interrupted. The specific behavior is then noted. Sometimes just making these observations can help parents and teachers understand what is going on in the autistic child's world.

The therapist then discusses specific areas where this child needs to improve and begins to work on one skill at a time. As the child masters one skill, the next one is introduced. Many persons who work with autistic children believe that a part of this teaching must include understanding why the child behaves the way she does so that the behavior is not replaced with another inappropriate behavior instead of a desired one. For example, if the child kicks and hits because he is scared to ride the bus, he may begin to

Research Project

The London Eye Mystery by Siobhan Dowd

The main character, Ted, is on the autism spectrum. He tries to solve the mystery of why his cousin disappeared from the London Ferris wheel.

ABA may be able to help a child with autism venture on to a school bus successfully.

scream instead if his fear is not addressed along with his kicking and hitting.

In the most intense ABA environment, discrete trial training is used. Each request from the therapist must **elicit** a response from the child and then a reaction from the therapist. Each task is broken down into small pieces and dealt with one at a time. This approach targets both unwanted behaviors and new skills that need to be created. ABA usually involves about thirty to forty hours of one-on-one work, along with training for all those who interact with the child.

The program strives to make the child's life consistent, filled with reinforcements for appropriate behavior.

Treatment and Education of Autistic and Related Communication Handicapped Children (TEACCH)

First begun in 1972 at the University of North Carolina, this statewide system provides various services to autistic persons and their families. The program runs on the premise that the environment should be adapted to the child with autism, not the child to the environment. The child's learning abilities are assessed through the Psycho Educational Profile (PEP), and teaching strategies are designed to improve communication, social, and coping skills. Through this system, children are taught to communicate their needs and feelings instead of acting them out—although in many cases the workers need to work at understanding the behavior in order to figure out why the child needs to behave this way. Usually, this means seeing the problem from the perspective of the autistic person. Through this understanding comes awareness of the cause of the behavior, and out of this awareness, intervention can be developed to change the behavior. In a structured environment, the child learns to adapt to new ways of meeting his needs. The system has been used in individual homes as well as by teachers in other states or countries.

Picture Exchange Communication Systems (PECS)

PECS was developed at the Delaware Autistic Program to allow persons with no verbal skills to communicate their needs and desires. Using ABA methods, persons exchange a picture for something they want. This may be an item such as a drink or a coat or an activity like swinging or going for a walk. One of the interesting things about this method is that the child initiates it. The reinforcement comes from

The TEACCH system designs educational strategies for each child with autism.

granting the child's desire immediately upon receiving the picture.

Floortime

Developed by child psychiatrist Stanley Greenspan, Floortime is based on six developmental sequences that are needed for children to move on to advanced learning. By encouraging children to move through these six stages, interaction is increased between child and adult. Following the child's lead allows the adult to encourage more of such interactions.

Social Stories

Developed by Carol Gray in 1991 to teach social skills, this program allows children to deal with situations through a story before they actually happen. By rehearsing situations that normally cause confusion and misunderstanding, the

A speech therapist may teach the word "ball" by handing the child an actual ball and repeating the word.

Text-Dependent Questions

1. Explain why IDEA is important for someone like Tucker.
2. What does an IEP include?
3. Explain why someone like Tucker might
   need a speech-language therapist.

child is able to better understand the appropriate response. The stories are written in first person and are specific to the needs of the child. Pictures or music may be used to help the child deal with her fears or needs. Much effort goes into trying to find the reasons why the child acts in the way she does in certain situations.

Speech Therapists or Speech-Language Pathologists

Speech therapists help children and adults with speech and language problems. Many times people with autism have trouble linking words to their meanings. Learning how to communicate is vitally important because many of their problem behaviors may actually be attempts to make others understand their world.

As a starting point, speech therapists associate words with pictures or the actual object. When teaching a child the word "ball," the therapist may show the child a ball, hand it to her, and say "ball."

Another way for children with autism to communicate may be for them to learn sign language. This does not mean the child will never talk orally, but sign language can provide a communication option that may lead to talking.

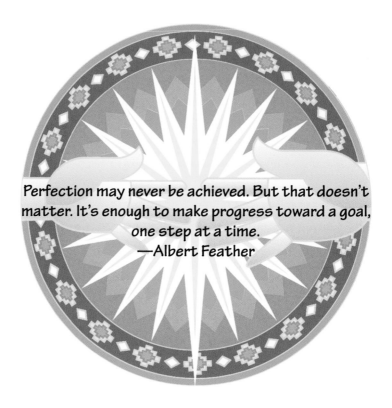

Perfection may never be achieved. But that doesn't matter. It's enough to make progress toward a goal, one step at a time.
—Albert Feather

Words to Understand

stimming: Unusual and often rhythmic body movements used by the autistic child to stimulate himself.

savant: A person who exhibits an exceptional amount of intellectual ability, especially in one particular field.

5

TWO STEPS FORWARD

L ivie's parents had two appointments the next week. The first was with Tucker's teacher and the school psychologist. The other meeting was with the director of the special education department at a college.

At the first meeting, the school psychologist told Mom and Dad that he and the teacher had discussed Tucker, trying to figure out the best way to work with him.

"As you know," the school psychologist said, "some of Tucker's behaviors are interfering with his learning experience. I've worked in some other school districts where we used a different behavioral method with students who have autism, and we have seen much success using this method. We were wondering if you would like to give it a try."

Livie's parents nodded and the school psychologist continued. "The basic idea is to observe the child's undesirable behaviors and actions before and after the behavior in order to try to understand why the child is doing that particular action. For example, a mother I once worked with complained that her day started out wrong because the first thing her son did every morning was empty his entire toy basket all over his bedroom floor. He repeated this behavior at different times during the day. She had tried everything she could think of to get him to stop. So I suggested that she watch what he did before and after the toy scattering. The mother noticed that her son looked around his room first but then immediately began emptying the basket. After the toys were all over, he found one toy that he then carried with him to other areas of the house. I suggested putting a floor shelf in his room with his toys lined up so he could see them. It did not take long before the child went to the shelf, picked out one toy, and left the others in place."

The therapist paused for a minute and then continued. "We have success with this in school settings when we have the parents' cooperation. The idea is that we change the environment to help the child—not change the child to fit the environment. So we need help observing the behavior and also carrying out the changes. It is much better if the autistic child's world is consistent. What we do here and what you do at home will work best if we are doing the same things."

The teacher talked about how Tucker's tantrums and throwing himself on the floor is disruptive in class and at home. They all agreed to start working with Tucker's tantrums.

That afternoon Mom and Dad explained to Livie how they needed to help Tucker's teacher.

"I can't always be there when Tucker begins a tantrum," Mom said. "So when you notice, you need to call me or watch to see what he does before and after."

"If this works and Tucker stops screaming so much, maybe we could go to the book fair at school next month. All of us together," Livie said hopefully.

Mom hugged Livie. "You will go to the book fair even if Tucker can't yet. But maybe we could do something fun together by the summer."

When Mom and Dad returned from the next meeting, the one at the college, they invited the whole extended family to their house. It would be the first family cookout of the year, and they had something to celebrate.

"We've finally found someone who has worked with Applied Behavior Analysis in a one-on-one setting. His name is Philip, and he's about twenty-four years old. He's worked with other autistic children and he's read all the literature, including the Lovaas studies and book," Mom told the gathering.

Livie and her cousins were running around the yard with bottles of bubbles, blowing rainbows of color that popped as they hit noses, hands, and toes. Even Uncle Mark had his own bottle and added to the fun. Livie paused long enough to listen.

"Philip will come three afternoons a week to start. He's a fairly serious young man and you can tell he believes in what he's doing."

"So now we have more homework," Dad added.

"I'll help!" Livie yelled.

"You might like this assignment," Mom said. "We have to make a whole list of things we would like Tucker to do and a whole list of things we would like him to stop doing."

"Put biting on the top of the 'don't do' list," Livie said.

Mom gave Tucker a few more pieces of hamburger. He liked them and ate well that night. He even looked at the pieces of cut-up fruit and reached for one, but he didn't put it in his mouth.

Dad took a bite of his hamburger. "We're getting a better vocabulary to talk about Tucker's behaviors. Like the way he rocks on that horse all the time, and the way he takes a cup and hits it on his teeth over and over and over—they call behaviors like that ***stimming***. They're self-stimulating behaviors that seem to help compensate for some of his sensory problems."

"I read that Temple Grandin, the woman who is autistic but now teaches at a university, used to rock back and forth," Mom put in. "It was one way she could shut out all the noise around her when she felt overwhelmed. She said that it was almost addictive, the more she rocked the more she wanted to rock." Mom buttered an ear of corn. "We need to pay more attention to Tucker's stimming, because some professionals believe if you can figure out what's causing the child stress or discomfort, you may be able to eliminate the self-stimulation."

Make Connections:
Consistency and Structure in the Environment

Developing a daily routine that an autistic child can count on has proven to be of great importance in the treatment of autism. When family life is disruptive, the incidence of problems such as self-injury, tantrums, and teasing other siblings increases.

Autistic children do not learn from experience in the same way that other children do. What happened last week doesn't teach them how to behave in the same situation this week. They seem to only learn and react to things they find are dependable, things that are always the same.

SELF-STIMULATORY ACTIONS

These are often very strange behaviors that autistic children do as a way to stimulate the senses that for them are out of control. Some children rock back and forth, others spin, walk on their toes, or grind their teeth. Others bang their heads or jump from foot to foot. Temple Grandin, an adult autistic, says that as a child she rocked or spun in circles in an effort to shut out what was going on around her. This behavior was addictive because the more she rocked the more she wanted to.

Most autistic children seem to "stim" more when they are anxious, stressed, or excited. Sometimes these behaviors can be used as a measure of how the child is feeling and may help a parent to know when he needs to intervene on behalf of the child.

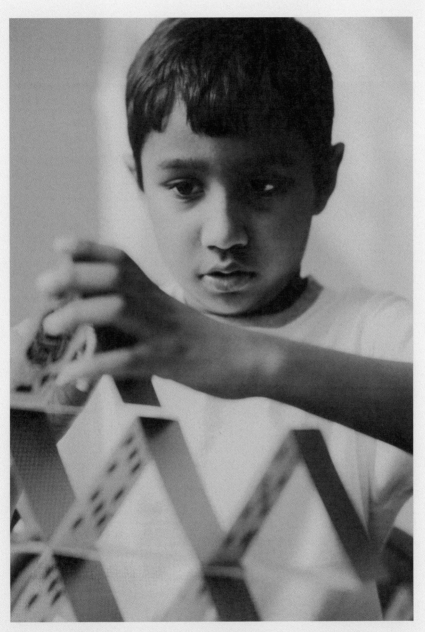

A child with autism may become intensely involved with objects, while avoiding interaction with human beings.

A small number of individuals with autism have "savant" skills that allow them to excel in music.

DIFFERENT KINDS OF AUTISM

Not everyone who has autism will have exactly the same symptoms. And there are variations in severity as well.

Low Function Versus High Function

A low-functioning person with autism might be completely nonverbal, have no personal relationships (even with parents and siblings), and possibly be self-abusive or aggressive. He may also have some degree of intellectual disability or problems with toileting and other basic self-care skills.

At the other end of the spectrum are those people with autism who are very high functioning. These individuals may never have even been diagnosed with autism, but they will have suffered through life with anxiety, depression, or obsessive-compulsive problems. And although they seem to cope, they have difficulty with relationships and are often the children who are teased, bullied, and left out by other children.

Both low-functioning autistics with *savant* skills and high-functioning autistic persons may excel in areas of music, math, or inventing things; they can perform at levels far above those without autism, perhaps because they are able to focus intently on one subject and think in ways that average persons may not. At any level, people with autism are very honest. They seem unable to tell a lie.

Asperger's Syndrome

Asperger's used to be a disorder on the autism spectrum, but the fifth edition of the Diagnostic and Statistical Manual of Mental Disorders (DSM-5) removed it in 2013.

Asperger's used to be seen as a subcategory of autism, and was more commonly diagnosed than autism. It is

Many children who had social and intellectual impairments were diagnosed with Asperger's until the DSM-5 removed the classification in 2013. Today, these children may be diagnosed as having autism spectrum disorder.

Research Project

***Mockingbird* by Kathryn Erskine**

This book will let you see how Caitlin, a girl on the autism spectrum, deals with a family tragedy.

Text-Dependent Questions

1. Explain why children on the autism spectrum need a reliable schedule.
2. What are self-stimulatory actions?
3. What does an IEP include?
4. Why did the most recent version of the DSM remove the Asperger's category?

classified as a somewhat milder form of a more severe disorder. Children diagnosed with this had great difficulty functioning socially; they were believed to be able to remember the smallest details about their fields of interest.

Today, the symptoms that used to be connected with Asperger's are included under the single diagnosis of autism spectrum disorder. Many people are not happy with the removal of Asperger's because those that are diagnosed with this disorder now do not have insurance coverage in certain states.

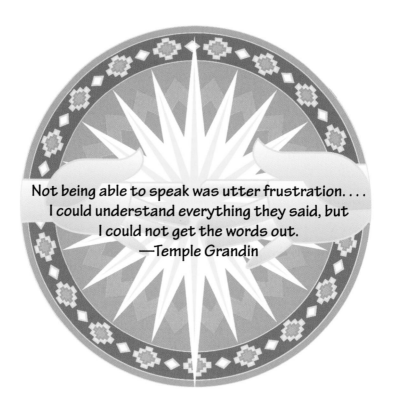

Not being able to speak was utter frustration. . . .
I could understand everything they said, but
I could not get the words out.
—Temple Grandin

Words to Understand

supplements: Vitamins or minerals taken in addition to regular foods in an effort to promote increased health.

hyperactivity: The condition of being more active than is usual or desirable.

gluten-free diet: A diet free of wheat, rye, and barley.

casein-free diet: A diet free of dairy products.

serotonin: An important chemical that affects certain neurological functions in the brain and body.

6

SUPPORT ALONG THE WAY

About two months later, Philip told Livie's mother about a chapter of the Autism Society of America that met near the college. He urged her to attend the next meeting the following week.

When Mom returned from the meeting, Livie was watching her favorite movie and eating popcorn. She listened to her mother say how glad she was that she went. Everyone there was willing to help. Mom opened her tote bag and pulled out pamphlets, a small book, a conference brochure, and about five pages of notes she took during the meeting.

"Tonight's speaker talked about *supplements*." Mom stacked all the literature in a neat pile on the table.

"You mean vitamins?" Dad asked.

"Yes. Quite a few parents give their children extra B_6 and magnesium. They say these supplements can improve attention and learning—maybe because they help decrease *hyperactivity* and irritability."

"I take vitamins," Livie put in. "Maybe Tucker needs to take some of them."

"These would be special vitamins made just for Tucker," Mom said. "But until Dad and I decide, you can see if Tucker would take one of your vitamins in the morning when you do."

"He'll probably just spit it out, even though they're Little Mermaid and taste like grapes."

Mom and Dad smiled. Livie felt happier tonight, not so angry about Tucker. One of the benefits of Tucker's afternoon sessions with Philip was that Tucker stayed occupied while Philip was there, and he was also more alert for a while afterward. He even seemed to be more content lately.

"I guess quite a few autistic children have problems with their digestive and immune systems," Mom said. "I remember reading about the **gluten-free diet**, the **casein-free diet**, and I think something about high amounts of yeast. There are just so many ideas out there. It's hard to know what will work and what's just wishful thinking."

"I find it hard to believe that a diet would do Tucker any good," Dad said.

Mom looked thoughtful. "It does make me wonder about allergies, though. You know how you feel every spring when the grass and trees start pollinating. Not only your nose and eyes, but your stomach bothers you and you're tired. Maybe Tucker inherited some of your allergies."

"And I don't concentrate as well when I'm feeling allergic," Dad agreed. "Do you think we need to try some of these diets?"

"We need to consider everything," Mom said. "The gentleman who spoke this evening suggested that even those children who show no bowel problems may have allergies. I just think we need to be open-minded. Next month there is going to be a conference and at the same time there will be a Sibshop meeting for the siblings of children with disabilities. Livie can go and meet other kids with siblings who have special needs."

Livie wasn't sure she wanted to. "Why can't I just stay home with Grandma?"

"Livie, I think this might be good for you. They have lots of fun. At this one they're going to play basketball and have a pizza party."

Livie stuck out her lip. "I don't want to!" She ran to her room and threw herself down on her bed.

Mom followed her and sat down next to her on the bed. She rubbed Livie's back. "Livie, you don't have to go, but everyone seems to think their children are really helped by the meetings."

"I'm tired of doing Tucker things."

"Then how about if we do more Livie things? Is there something special you want to do?"

"I want to take art lessons. Ellie takes them, and she brings the things she makes to school to show the teacher."

"That sounds like fun. I never thought of it, but I'll talk to Dad."

Livie sat up. "And if you really want me to go with you to that meeting, I will."

"How about just you and I go? We'll do some shopping and eat supper out and make a whole day of it."

Philip came every afternoon now, and Tucker was beginning to respond in small ways. He looked at Mom once when she entered the family room. It was only for a few seconds but his eyes met hers. Another time when they were in the backyard, the neighbor's dogs ran by, chasing each other. Tucker lifted his hand and pointed.

"Look! Tucker's pointing at the dogs," Mom shouted. "Livie, look."

Dad walked over close to Tucker. "Dog, good showing dog." Dad bent down and looked into Tucker's face.

Livie looked up from where she was drawing flowers at the picnic table. "Dad, you sound just like Philip when he's teaching Tucker."

Dad smiled and looked down at Livie's drawing. "Wow, Livie, that's a beautiful picture."

The next week Livie's parents asked her if she wanted to be in the room while Philip worked with Tucker. So Livie sat quietly in the corner of the living room and listened.

Philip showed Tucker a cow. "Cow," Philip said. He put the cow back on the table with the other animals. "Give me cow."

"Mom, won't it be cool when Tucker can talk?" Livie whispered.

Mom wiped her eyes with the back of her hand. "I can't wait until he can talk. Until he can ask for what he wants and until he looks right at me and says 'Mom.'"

Mom and Livie enjoyed their day out. The conference was a great source of information, but best of all, Mom made another friend. Val was an elderly woman whose grandson hadn't been diagnosed with autism until his eighth birthday. He had had terrible seizures as a baby, and for the first year of his life they wondered if he would even live. These complications led doctors to investigate many avenues. Mom told us Val's grandson had some intellectual disability, social problems, and still didn't speak, even though he was eighteen now.

"But Val has spent years learning everything she can about autism. She has newsletters and books, and she has taken lots of notes. Best of all, she lives only about a half an hour from here."

"Sounds like you've met another good friend," Dad said, "someone who's had a lot of care issues we haven't had to deal with yet." He turned to Livie. "And what about you, Miss Livie, how was your day?"

"We had a great time, Dad." Livie squeezed Mom's hand. "Do you want to see my new summer clothes?"

"Of course I do. We'll have a fashion show. And what about your special meeting with the kids, the Sibshop?"

"It was fun, just like Mom said. We played basketball and ate pizza, and we even talked a little about our brothers and sisters. They called them 'special needs' kids. Some of the kids there have it harder than we do. And you know what else? It doesn't really matter anyway because they're all just like me. They love their brother or sister, even if they're a pain lots of the time."

THE SIBLINGS OF CHILDREN WITH AUTISM

Sibshops

The Sibling Support Project began in Seattle, Washington, and has spread to thirty-eight other states, offering a place where the needs of brothers and sisters of children with special needs are recognized and addressed. The following are some of the things that happen at these important gatherings:

- Fun is the main goal. At least half of the session is devoted to games, arts, or recreation.
- Communication with the kids who attend is based on the realization that brothers and sisters share the same concerns as the parents. What's more, brothers and sisters have unique concerns as well. Kids are taught that there is no right or wrong way to feel about their particular situation. Brothers and sisters may have the longest-lasting relationship with the special needs person, so it is important to build these relationships.
- Sibshops provide a place where the sibling can say whatever she needs to without worrying if she is hurting someone's feelings.
- Sibshops help siblings see beyond the disabilities of their brothers and sisters and focus on the positive aspects of life with them.
- Sibshops help answer siblings' specific questions, like how to deal with kids who bully their brother or sister with special needs. They address feelings of jealousy and loneliness, because siblings may feel they are not as important to their parents as their special needs sibling, as well as feelings of resentment and frustration on the part of those who have to spend a great deal of time dealing with the needs of their sibling.

Having a sibling with autism can be difficult. Sibshops and other forms of support for kids can help.

Make Connections: Keeping Siblings Informed

 Helping siblings understand what is going on in the life of their autistic brother or sister may be the most important job of the parents. In order to help keep the family as healthy as possible, siblings should be monitored as regularly as their autistic brother or sister. Information should be geared to the age of the sibling and should be simple enough for them to understand why certain decisions are made.

Siblings of children with autism may become super achievers to gain more attention in the home. Or they may begin negative pursuits, hoping Mom and Dad will take notice. These siblings often feel they miss out on the extras, like music lessons, help with college tuition, and special vacations. The cost for care and education of the child with autism can be staggering, leaving little resources left over for other family members. Some government officials are asking the government to initiate programming to help families like these.

AUTISM SOCIETY OF AMERICA

In 1965, a small group of parents organized to form the Autism Society of America (ASA). These parents originally worked from their homes, but today the society boasts a membership of over 50,000. Along with providing information and referrals, the society represents those with autism throughout the country by promoting public awareness and research.

One of the most exciting aspects of the society is its local chapters. There, persons seeking help with the day-to-day concerns of an autistic child can benefit from others' personal experience and get resources to find the necessary

A child with autism often prefers to play by herself rather than with other children.

trained professionals to help manage each child's treatment. Local conferences and seminars teach about education, nutrition, and other important issues.

Because the ASA realizes that each autistic person is an individual and believes no single program or treatment will benefit all individuals with autism, members work with the family and the autistic person to help plan what will work best for them. What might work well for one person may only have minimal effects for another.

The mission of the Autism Society of America is to promote lifelong access and opportunity for all individuals within the autism spectrum, and their families, to be fully participating members of their community. Education, advocacy at state and federal levels, active public awareness, and the promotion of research form the cornerstones of ASA's efforts to carry forth its mission.

The reality of a child with autism is very different from that of other children.

Some people believe that vitamin supplements may provide help for children with autism.

TREATING AUTISM WITH NUTRITION

Vitamin Supplements

Research and tests have been done using large doses of vitamin B_6 and magnesium to treat children with autism. Bernard Rimland, who founded the Autism Research Institute in San Diego and passed away in 2006, believed that the use of B_6 and magnesium megavitamin therapy produces improvement in attention and learning and decreases hyperactivity and irritability. Studies have shown that a number of autistic children have high blood levels of **serotonin**; the vitamins may work to adjust these levels, accounting for the changes in behavior. Not all scientists are convinced that this therapy can actually reduce autism symptoms.

Leaky Gut Theory—Casein-Free/Gluten-Free Diet

During the mid 1970s, researcher Jak Panksepp studied the abnormal reaction to gluten and casein in children suffering

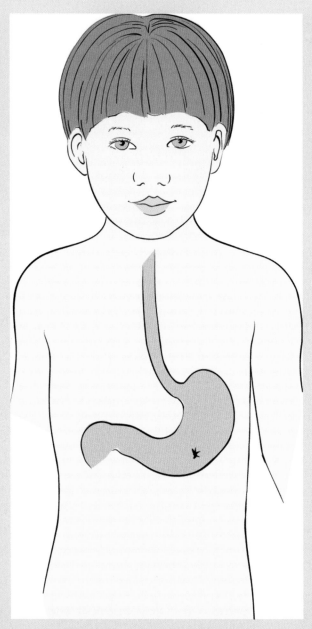

According to the leaky gut theory, children with autism do not properly digest grains and dairy products.

Research Project

Rules by Cynthia Lord

This Newbery Honor book tells the story of Catherine, who—like Livie—must learn to understand and accept a little brother with autism.

with autism. These proteins found in wheat, rye, and barley (gluten) and dairy products (casein) are broken down in the stomach into amino acids called opioid peptides. These amino acids have a structure similar to morphine and are highly toxic.

For normal persons, these opioids are flushed from the system, but Panksepp believed that autistic children have a problem with the wall of their stomach that allows the opioids to leak into the bloodstream and into the brain, where they cause damage. From there, they are flushed out of the bloodstream through urine by way of the kidneys.

Some studies show that children with autism have higher levels of the opioid peptides in their urine. This would only be true if the peptides had been in the bloodstream instead of being flushed through the digestive system, proving Panksepp's theory. However, not all autistics have the high levels in their urine.

Some people advocate a casein-free, gluten-free diet for autistic children, but this treatment is still controversial. Again, may scientists do not feel that the research adequately supports this treatment approach.

To dream of the reality you want is
to waste the reality that exists.
—Anonymous

7

LEARNING IN A NEW WAY

Tucker continued in school throughout the summer, and Philip still came every afternoon. Tucker was beginning to say words he had not spoken since he was a toddler. He also added new words, some that Philip taught him and some he seemed to learn on his own or at school.

Tucker's teacher was pleased with his progress. He had fewer tantrums, and he sat at his desk or on the floor without disrupting the class. As they worked together, more of Tucker's time was directed to positive activities, and everyone could see a difference both in school and at home.

Livie enjoyed her summer pool party. She spent a lot of time with her cousins, and the summer passed quickly.

By the beginning of September Tucker was putting a few words together. One day Livie's father and Tucker headed for some play in the backyard.

"Tell Mom bye," Dad said as they headed out the door.

Tucker looked at Mom and said, "Bye, bye, Mom."

"Bye-bye, Tucker."

Mom and Dad and Livie smiled at each other.

By his fourth birthday, Tucker was able to help Mom as she dressed him in the morning before school. He ate more foods and often sat in the middle of the family room closer to everyone as they talked, watched television, or played games. He even began playing with toys, driving trucks along the floor. But he still loved his collection of cups. He had a little bag that he carried around the house filled with different cups. He stacked them and rolled them across the kitchen floor.

When he was learning colors, Livie helped. "Orange." She held up an orange cup. She picked up a green one. "Green." She set the cups next to each other on the table.

Tucker pointed at the green cup.

"Green," Livie said again.

"Green," Tucker said.

Livie handed him the green cup. "Good green, Tucker. Good green."

Tucker looked at Livie and reached out to touch her hand. Livie put her hand on his and then picked up the orange cup.

"Orange."

Without any prompting, Tucker had reached out to touch Livie!

Mom's friend Val had gotten Tucker a magnetic set of letters that they put on the lower front of the refrigerator. Val had told Mom that her grandson Alex used a letter board to spell out things he was trying to say to them. One day while they were at church, the choir director was asking the members to choose their favorite songs to sing. Alex, who was about fifteen at the time, sat between his mom and his grandmother. He began pointing to letters on the board. Val watched as he spelled out "Jesus Loves Me." They were amazed that he had understood what was going on and that he could spell. Val insisted they had not taught him to spell words; he just seemed to know how they were spelled.

When she gave Tucker the letters, Val said, "Now young man, let's see what you can do with these letters."

Livie loved to sit in front of the refrigerator, spelling little messages. She wrote, "I love you," "Tucker is a boy," and "spring is here" on one particularly warm March day. Tucker would stop sometimes and watch when he saw Livie spelling refrigerator words.

"Look, Tucker, here's the letters for cup. C-U-P. Cup."

Philip went away for a week visiting relatives. While he was gone, he attended a one-day seminar on Applied Behavioral Analysis. Dr. Ivar Lovaas and one of his supervisors spoke about suggestions for furthering an existing program. Philip came back with lots of ideas and began incorporating them into Tucker's sessions.

One of these was identifying the plural and singular. Philip began by using Tucker's cups.

"Cup." Philip put one cup onto the table.

"Cup," Tucker said.

"One cup," Philip said.

"One cup," Tucker reached for the cup.

"Cup down." Philip put another cup on the table next to it. He picked up both cups. "Two cups."

Tucker just watched. And so Philip went over one cup and two cups again and again until Tucker understood.

Livie, who loved to play school, continued the game of refrigerator letters. She would call to Tucker, insisting that he come to play. Most of the time he watched from a distance, but occasionally he sat by her, looking as though he were enjoying the game. She always spelled C-U-P at some point during their playtime.

Then one day Tucker stopped at the refrigerator himself. He touched one of the letters. Another day Livie saw him move a few more letters. Finally the day came when Tucker walked to the refrigerator and set two of his cups on the floor. He moved the letters around and when he walked away the word C-U-P-S was on the front of the refrigerator.

"Mom, he did it. Tucker spelled cup. No he spelled 'cups.' But I don't know what to say. I've never heard Philip say 'good spell cups.'"

Mom, Dad, and Philip talked about what this could mean. Mom told Tucker's teacher at their next meeting at school.

When Mom told Val, they hugged. Val just kept saying, "Aren't they amazing? What workers they are, trying to learn these new things. I'm so proud of you, Tucker."

Everyone guessed that somehow Tucker had learned from Livie's spelling class and Philip's teaching on plurals to spell C-U-P-S. But best of all they knew he was improving, and now everyone began to have hope for what Tucker might do next.

MEDICAL PROBLEMS

Children with autism have increased chances of developing the following medical problems:

- Seizures occur in as many as one in three children with autism. Sometimes they do not develop until adolescence. They are caused by abnormal electrical activity in the brain. During a seizure, the person may lose consciousness, bladder or bowel control, move in unusual ways, or stare into space.
- Injuries may occur more often because of poor judgment, a lack of fear, or poor motor skills. Providing a safe environment is key to caring for someone with autism. Those who suffer from self-abusive tendencies such as head banging, scratching, or hand biting must be carefully monitored for infection or fractures.
- Infections are sometimes more difficult to treat because the child may not cooperate with treatment. He may not be able to tell of pain in specific areas so observation of any changes in behavior or indications of pain needs to be monitored.
- Dental care may be difficult because the brush may hurt as the child brushes. Being aware of why he does not want to brush and trying different brushes or toothpastes may help. Selecting a dentist who takes the time to help the child understand what is happening will help ease fears.
- Nutrition often is a problem for children with autism because of their desire to keep things the same. Some will select just a few foods and refuse to eat anything else. Sometimes certain food textures or tastes will cause a tantrum. This can become a problem

bordering on malnutrition. Another problem can develop with those children who overeat. Food may be a way they gain some relief and happiness. If the problem becomes severe, testing and observation by a dietician may be needed.

- Allergies, eczema, and asthma are also more prevalent in autistic children. This complicates life with medications and can cause other problems including impaired breathing and infections, and in general makes it more difficult to help a child who isn't always able to share how he feels.

Medications

The FDA has not approved a medication as a treatment for autism. And although there are no drugs that cure autism,

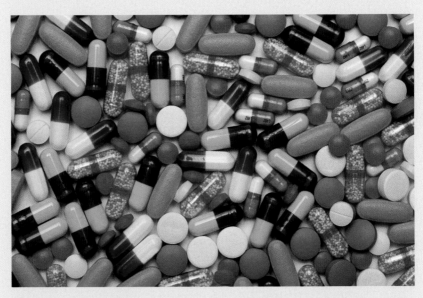

No pill can cure autism—but some can ease the more troubling symptoms.

some may be used to help relieve or reduce symptoms and behaviors that produce problems for the person and his family. These drugs were developed for other conditions but have been successful in treating some autistic symptoms like attention difficulties, hyperactivity, self-abusive behavior, hand biting, and anxiety. Choosing to use medication is very individualistic as is all treatment for autism, but the goal must be to help the person enjoy a more healthy life—not getting rid of autism itself.

Here are some of the medications that may be prescribed for children to help with symptoms:

1. Antipsychotic medications: these are more commonly used to treat serious medical illnesses, such as schizophrenia. These medicines may help reduce aggression and other serious behavioral problems in children, including children with ASD. They may also help reduce repetitive behaviors, hyperactivity, and attention problems.

2. Antidepressant Medications: these include fluoxetine (Prozac) or sertraline (Zoloft), and are usually prescribed to treat depression and anxiety but are sometimes prescribed to reduce repetitive behaviors. Some antidepressants may also help control aggression and anxiety in children with autism. However, researchers still are not sure if these medications are useful; a recent study suggested that the antidepressant citalopram (Celexa) was no more effective than a placebo (sugar pill) at reducing repetitive behaviors in children with ASD.

3. Stimulant Medications: these include methylphenidate (Ritalin), and are safe and effective in treating people with attention deficit hyperactivity disorder (ADHD). Methylphenidate has been shown to effectively treat

A child with autism may enjoy simple, repetitive tasks.

hyperactivity in children with ASD as well. But not as many children with ASD respond to treatment, and those who do have shown more side effects than children with ADHD and not ASD.

DISCIPLINE ISSUES

Because autistic children do not reason the same way that other children do, discipline often becomes a problem. When a sibling misbehaves, he can be punished by any number of means, including a time out, being sent to his room, or taking away a favorite activity. Autistic children, however, need to be reinforced for positive behavior or be taught how to replace misbehavior with a positive action.

Siblings may not understand why their brother or sister with autism has different consequences for misbehavior than they do.

Make Connections: Emergency Information

Persons with autism may not be able to help themselves if they get into situations where they are lost, in an accident, or during other emergencies. Bracelets may be worn to help identify specific health problems; these will include the home phone number, medical contact information, and information about the person (for example, the fact that she is nonverbal, what medications she takes, or any other necessary information).

This may be difficult for the sibling to understand at first; he may not feel it is fair that he is "punished" while the child with autism is rewarded. As always, information about autism and how the sibling with special needs is affected by it is the best way to deal with a child who feels things are unfair when it comes to discipline.

One of the difficulties for autistic persons is that they do not look like they are disabled. They look very normal; they usually do not wear a leg brace or sit in a wheelchair. So when they go out in public, people do not feel there is any excuse for their misbehavior. The result is that parents are

Research Project

The Curious Incident of the Dog in the Night-Time by Mark Haddon

This mystery is told from the point of view of a young man with autism.

Text-Dependent Questions

1. Why are injuries and infections more likely to occur to children with autism?
2. Explain why many children with autism have nutrition problems.

thought to have done a poor job disciplining them, and the children are believed to be acting out on purpose, meaning they are just "bad" kids.

EMERGENCY INFORMATION

Persons with autism may not be able to help themselves if they get into situations where they are lost, in an accident, or during other emergencies. Bracelets may be worn to help identify specific health problems; these will include the home phone number, medical contact information, and information about the person (for example, the fact that she is nonverbal, what medications she takes, or any other necessary information).

Even the worst situation carries the
chance for a happy change.
—Euripides

Words to Understand

behavior modification: A technique for changing behavior by reinforcing appropriate behaviors and
extinguishing undesired behaviors.
mainstreamed: To have placed a child with special
needs in regular school classes.
task-oriented: Concentrating effort on the outcome
of a particular task.

8

LOOKING FORWARD TO TUCKER'S FUTURE

By Tucker's fifth birthday, the whole family was involved in *behavior modification*. Even Grandpa praised Tucker one day for asking for a cup of juice.

"Good, ask for juice, Tucker. Good, ask for juice." Grandpa poured juice into one of Tucker's cups.

Tucker was talking in short sentences and beginning to notice when family members came and went from a room. Dad, Mom, and Livie had even started visiting with him at other homes. One day as they arrived at Grandma's, Tucker ran toward her and reached up his arms. Grandma cried as she hugged him.

Mom decided to have a birthday party. She would invite the family, Val, Anita and Carl, and a little boy who lived on the next street. Mom and the boy's mother had become friends. The boy's mother was especially helpful and encouraged her son to interact with Tucker. One day last week the two boys were playing with cars, and Tucker actually walked to where the boy sat.

"Red car." Tucker held out the car to his neighbor.

Mom held her breath. Tucker never shared anything with anyone, other than herself and Livie.

"Thanks." The boy took the car and began driving it into his play garage. He handed Tucker one of his yellow trucks.

"Yellow truck." Tucker sat down next to the boy.

The day of the party came at last. Mom had bought a cake, ice cream, balloons, dinosaur plates, napkins, and cups. She had wrapped a few presents for Tucker and placed them on the table. While she prepared some food, Tucker climbed onto a kitchen chair. He reached for one of the presents.

"Look, Nate. Get the camera. Tucker, open birthday present."

Tucker began ripping the paper off a large plastic dinosaur.

"Dino, green dino," Tucker said.

Mom cried and laughed and hugged Tucker. "Good, green dinosaur, Tucker. Good, green dinosaur."

The rest of the day was wonderful. Everyone had fun. Even Carl seemed to enjoy the cake and only screamed once when his mother wanted to take off his jacket. Livie showed everyone her latest artwork. And Tucker played with his dinosaur and smiled whenever someone handed him a gift.

The following year, Tucker was **mainstreamed** into some classes at the kindergarten level. He was doing simple math, reading, and spelling. Philip continued coming until Tucker was eight years old, when everyone agreed Tucker was able to use his skills in most situations without a lot of help. Not having Philip each day was strange, but he visited regularly.

Tucker still did not like change. Each year, Mom and Dad met with Tucker's teachers and the rest of his IEP team to help them realize what Tucker needed to continue to be successful in school. One teacher in sixth grade took a special interest in him and was able to tell by looking at Tucker if he was having a problem relating to changes going on in the classroom. She even devised a card system that Tucker could use so that he felt safe in asking for help.

Except for the neighbor boy Matt, Tucker had very few friends. Most children could not understand how Tucker functioned. He did not always look at them when he talked. He also was very **task-oriented**, so he often paid more attention to what he was doing instead of who he was doing it with. He went to school, though, and kept up with the work. Although he was two years behind his age group, he had little trouble dealing with the academics at school. He had even begun to take art lessons with Livie. He was pretty good, Livie thought, and they enjoyed sharing the time together.

Tucker didn't go to sports games—they were too loud and confusing—but he did help at the church car washes. He didn't participate in the school play, but he helped paint the backgrounds and collect props. Mom and Dad sent him to a special camp each summer, where the staff continued working on his social skills in a new environment, a kind of social conditioning.

Sometimes, Mom, Dad, and Livie talked about what Tucker would do when he grew up. They hoped he would be able to go to college to get a job that required his educational skills and not so much social skill. They worried, but they also knew there were lots of alternatives. Tucker would hopefully be able to live on his own and support himself.

"Hi, Livie." Tucker said.

"How are you, Tucker?" Livie went into his room. "What are you doing?"

"Oh, just looking at the cups. How about this cup that Aunt Emma sent me from Iran? It's pretty cool, isn't it? Do you know that back in 435 B.C. being a cupbearer in the Persian court was a great honor? The cupbearer spent lots of time with the king. He usually held the cup in his left hand and carried a napkin for the king to wipe his lips on his left shoulder."

"Hey, Tucker, you've told me that story before." Livie laughed.

"Oh, yeah. Should we be having a two-way conversation? How's your watercolor painting?"

"Great, thanks. I'm doing one very large painting and one miniature one. It's really fun. Have you been working on yours?"

"Yep, but we're doing pastels. I like them but they are messy." He set down the cup. "I like to keep the plastics and especially the ones from fast food places to remind me of how far I've come. Remember when I loved to get a cup from Burger King and I hated to let anyone else touch it?"

"I sure do. And I remember a whole lot more. I love you, Tucker."

Make Connections: Coping with Autism

"Autism means having to watch how I feel every second that I am awake. Autism means having challenges when I leave the room fearing that others will say unkind things about me to other people. Autism means being dateless on weekends as well as constant loneliness, only watching TV on Saturday night. Autism means not being able to fit in on social peer relations. However, autism in my case means that I have a calendar memory for birthdays, being articulate and having skills. I, all in all, would rather be autistic than normal."
—*Therese Marie Ronan*

EFFECTS OF NATIONAL VIOLENCE ON AUTISTIC CHILDREN IN THE CLASSROOM

One of the outcomes of the effort to reduce violence in many areas of the nation is that autistic children who show verbal or physical aggression are losing many of their rights to a free and appropriate education. Although violence exhibited by these children is part of their disability, not conscious misconduct, it may still result in suspensions from school and sometimes arrests.

AUTISM RESEARCH INSTITUTE

The Autism Research Institute (ARI) was established in 1967. Methods of preventing, diagnosing, and treating autism are studied at the institute, and this research is then shared with parents and professionals worldwide.

AUTISTIC SAVANTS

Autistic persons with savant qualities have extraordinary abilities in certain subjects, achieving a level of performance that most people could never reach. These areas might include math, memory, music, or art. The percentage of savants within the autistic population is 10 percent, while in the general public it is only one percent. If a person is savant in math he may be able to figure the answer to a difficult multiplication problem without using a calculator. A person with savant music skills may be able to play back an entire classical piece after hearing it only once. The movie *Rain Man* brought knowledge about autistic savants to the general population when Dustin Hoffman played the part of an autistic brother with savant abilities.

A child with autism may prefer being alone in his room to spending time with the rest of the family.

Some autistic savants have an uncanny ability to manipulate numbers.

LOOKING TOWARD THE FUTURE

Independent Living

Some facilities have been established to provide indepen-
dent, supervised, or assisted living for persons with special
needs, including autistic teens and adults. Some of the
available services include:

- day programs
- vocational activities
- recreation

- relief services and care for families who need to be away from the autistic person for any length of time
- management help by way of education and/or medication

Many of these facilities are farms where people with autism work to provide for themselves, learn to substitute appropriate actions for undesired behavior, and enjoy the fruits of their labor by way of food, craftsmanship, and animal care.

With the continued desire to promote independence, more and more opportunities are being developed to fulfill this expectation.

Hope

Although autism is a lifelong condition, author Uta Frith has this to say:

Autistic people can, and often do, compensate for their handicap to a remarkable degree. They may be guided to a niche in society where their assets are put to good use. They may remain at home as helpful companions to aging parents who understand them. There are less favorable outcomes. However, one must remember that to predict the future of an individual autistic child is just as uncertain as it is in the case of a normal child.

Dr. Michael Powers concludes *Children with Autism* with these words:

One final message—a message that is too often forgotten by parents in the day-to-day struggle and frustration of raising a child with autism. There is hope.

Research Project

Episodes: Scenes from Life, Love, and Autism by Blaze Ginsberg

This an autobiography was written by a teenager.

Not all children with autism will gain the communication skills that Tucker did—but some will. Each child with autism is different, and each will have different developmental achievements. Autism is a lifelong disability that has no "cure." Early intervention, however, can help each child with autism reach his full potential.

Text-Dependent Questions

1. What does the Autistic Research Institute do?
2. Explain what an "autistic savant" is.
3. Can autism be cured?

FURTHER READING

Barron, Judy, and Sean Barron. *There's a Boy in Here.* New York: Simon & Schuster, 2002.

Cohen, Shirley. *Targeting Autism.* Berkeley: University of California Press, 2006.

Grandin, Temple and Richard Panek. *The Autistic Brain: Thinking Across the Spectrum.* New York: Houghton Mifflin Harcourt Publishing Company, 2013.

Ives, Martine, and Nell Munro. *Caring for a Child with Autism.* London and Philadelphia, Pa.: Jessica Kingsley, 2002.

Robison, John Elder. *Look Me in the Eye: My Life with Asperger's.* New York: Broadway, 2007.

Wing, Lorna. *The Autistic Spectrum.* Berkeley, Calif.: Ulysses, 2003.

FOR MORE INFORMATION

The ARC of the United States
www.thearc.org

Autism Research Institute
www.autism.com

Autism Society of America
www.autism-society.org

Autism Speaks
www.autismspeaks.org

TEACCH Autism Program
www.teacch.com

The Doug Flutie Jr. Foundation for Autism, Inc.
www.dougflutiejrfoundation.org

The Dan Marino Foundation
www.danmarinofoundation.org

Families for Early Autism Treatment (FEAT)
www.feat.org

Lovaas Institute
www.lovaas.com

Publisher's Note:

The websites listed on these pages were active at the time of publication. The publisher is not responsible for websites that have changed their address or discontinued operation since the date of publication. The publisher will review and update the websites upon each reprint.

SERIES GLOSSARY
OF KEY TERMS

Accessibility: An environment that allows people with disabilities to participate as much as they can.

Accommodation: A change in how a student receives instruction, without substantially changing the instructional content.

Achievement test: A standardized test that measures a student's performance in academic areas such as math, reading, and writing.

Acting out: Behavior that's inappropriate within the setting.

Adaptive behavior: The extent to which an individual is able to adjust to and apply new skills to new environments, tasks, objects, and people.

Ambulatory: Able to walk independently.

American Sign Language (ASL): A language based on gestures that is used by people who are deaf in the United States and Canada.

Americans with Disabilities Act (ADA): In 1990, Congress passed this act, which provides people who have disabilities with the same freedoms as Americans who do not have disabilities. The law addresses access to buildings and programs, as well as housing and employment.

Anxiety: An emotional state of fear, often not attached to any direct threat, which can cause sweating, increased pulse, and breathing difficulty.

Aphasia: Loss of the ability to speak.

Articulation: The ability to express oneself through sounds, words, and sentences.

Asperger syndrome: An disorder that is on the autism spectrum, which can cause problems with nonverbal learning disorder and social interactions.

Assessment: The process of collecting information about a student's learning needs through tests, observations, and interviewing the student, the family, and others. Assistive technology: Any item or piece of equipment that is used to improve the capabilities of a child with a disability.

Attention-deficit/hyperactivity Disorder (ADHD): A disorder that can cause inappropriate behavior, including poor attention skills, impulsivity, and hyperactivity.

Autism spectrum disorder: A range of disabilities that affect verbal and nonverbal communication and social interactions.

Bipolar disorder: A brain disorder that causes uncontrollable changes in moods, behaviors, thoughts, and activities.

Blind (legally): Visual acuity for distance vision of 20/200 or less in the better eye after best correction with conventional lenses; or a visual field of no greater than 20 degrees in the better eye.

Bullying: When a child faces threats, intimidation, name-calling, gossip, or physical violence.

Cerebral palsy (CP): Motor impairment caused by brain damage during birth or before birth. It can be mild to severe, does not get worse, and cannot be cured. Chronic: A condition that persists over a long period of time.

Cognitive: Having to do with remembering, reasoning, understanding, and using judgment.

Congenital: Any condition that is present at birth.

Counseling: Advice or help through talking, given by someone qualified to give such help.

Deaf: A hearing loss so severe that speech cannot be understood, even with a hearing aid, even if some sounds may still be perceived.

Developmental: Having to do with the steps or stages in growth and development of a child.

Disability: A limitation that interferes with a person's ability to walk, hear, talk, or learn.

Down syndrome: An abnormal chromosomal condition that changes the development of the body and brain, often causing intellectual disabilities.

Early intervention: Services provided to infants and toddlers ages birth to three who are at risk for or are showing signs of having a slower than usual development.

Emotional disturbance (ED): An educational term (rather than psychological) where a student's inability to build or maintain satisfactory interpersonal relationships with peers and teachers, inappropriate types of behavior or feelings, and moods of unhappiness or depression get in the way of the student being able to learn and function in a school setting.

Epilepsy: A brain disorder where the electrical signals in the brain are disrupted, causing seizures. Seizures can cause brief changes in a person's body movements, awareness, emotions, and senses (such as taste, smell, vision, or hearing).

Fine motor skills: Control of small muscles in the hands and fingers, which are needed for activities such as writing and cutting.

Gross motor skills: Control of large muscles in the arms, legs, and torso, which are needed for activities such as running and walking.

Hard-of-hearing: A hearing loss that may affect the student's educational performance.

Heredity: Traits acquired from parents.

Individualized Education Plan (IEP): A written education plan for students ages 5 to 22 with disabilities, developed by a team of professionals, (teachers, therapists, etc.) and the child's parent(s), which is reviewed and updated yearly. It contains a description of the child's level of development, learning needs, goals and objectives, and services the child will receive.

Individuals with Disabilities Education Act (IDEA): The Individuals with Disabilities Education Act (IDEA) is the nation's federal special education law that requires public schools to serve the educational needs of students with disabilities. IDEA requires that schools provide special education services to eligible students as outlined in a student's IEP, and it also provides very specific requirements to guarantee a free appropriate education for students with disabilities in the least restrictive environment.

Intervention: A planned activity to increase students' skills.

Learning disability: A general term for specific kinds of learning problems that can cause a person to have challenges learning and using certain skills, such as reading, writing, listening, speaking, reasoning, and doing math.

Least restrictive environment: The educational setting or program that provides a student with as much contact as possible with children without disabilities, while still appropriately meeting all of the child's learning and physical needs.

Mainstreaming: Providing any services, including education, for children with disabilities, in a setting with other children who do not have disabilities.

Motor: Having to do with muscular activity.

Nonambulatory: Not able to walk independently.

Occupational therapist (OT): A professional who helps individuals be able to handle meaningful activities of daily life such as self-care skills, education, recreation, work or social interaction.

Palate: The roof of the mouth.

Paraplegia: Paralysis of the legs and lower part of the body.

Partially sighted: A term formally used to indicate visual acuity of 20/70 to 20/200, but also used to describe visual impairment in which usable vision is present.

Pediatrics: The medical treatment of children.

Physical therapist (PT): A person who helps individuals improve the use of bones, muscles, joints, and/or nerves.

Prenatal: Existing or occurring prior to birth.

Quadriplegia: Paralysis affecting all four limbs.

Referral: In special education, students are referred for screening and evaluation to see if they are eligible for special education services.

Self-care skills: The ability to care for oneself; usually refers to basic habits of dressing, eating, etc.

Special Education: Specialized instruction made to fit the unique learning strengths and needs of each student with disabilities in the least restrictive environment.

Speech impaired: Communication disorder such as stuttering, impaired articulation, a language impairment, or a voice impairment, which adversely affects a child's educational performance.

Speech pathologist: A trained therapist, who provides treatment to help a person develop or improve articulation, communication skills, and oral-motor skills.

Spina bifida: A problem that happens in the first month of pregnancy when the spinal column doesn't close completely.

Standardized tests: Tests that use consistent directions, procedures, and criteria for scoring, which are often administered to many students in many schools across the country.

Stereotyping: A generalization in which individuals are falsely assigned traits they do not possess based on race, ethnicity, religion, disability, or gender.

Symptom: An observable sign of an illness or disorder.

Syndrome: A set of symptoms that occur together.

Therapy: The treatment or application of different techniques to improve specific conditions for curing or helping to live with various disorders.

Traumatic Brain Injury (TBI): Physical damage to the brain that could result in physical, behavioral, or mental changes depending on which area of the brain is injured.

Visually impaired: Any degree of vision loss that affects an individual's ability to perform the tasks of daily life, which is caused by a visual system that is not working properly or not formed correctly.

Vocational education: Educational programs that prepare students for paid or unpaid employment, or which provide additional preparation for a career that doesn't require a college degree.

INDEX

ABOUT THE AUTHOR
AND THE CONSULTANTS

Sherry Bonnice has also written several books for three other Mason Crest series: CA-REERS WITH CHARACTER, NORTH AMERICAN FOLKLORE, and PSYCHIATRIC DISORDERS: DRUGS AND PSYCHOLOGY FOR THE MIND AND BODY.

Dr. Lisa Albers is a developmental behavioral pediatrician at Children's Hospital Boston and Harvard Medical School, where her responsibilities include outpatient pediatric teaching and patient care in the Developmental Medicine Center. She currently is Director of the Adoption Program, Director of Fellowships in Developmental and Behavioral Pediatrics, and collaborates in a consultation program for community health centers. She is also the school consultant for the Walker School, a residential school for children in the state foster-care system.

Dr. Carolyn Bridgemohan is an instructor in pediatrics at Harvard Medical School and is a board-certified developmental behavioral pediatrician on staff in the Developmental Medicine Center at Children's Hospital Boston. Her clinical practice includes children and youth with autism, hearing impairment, developmental language disorders, global delays, intellectual disabilities, and attention and learning disorders. Dr. Bridgemohan is coeditor of *Bright Futures Case Studies for Primary Care Clinicians: Child Development and Behavior*, a curriculum used nationwide in pediatric residency training programs.

Cindy Croft is the State Special Needs Director in Minnesota, coordinating Project EXCEPTIONAL MN, through Concordia University. Project EXCEPTIONAL MN is a state project that supports the inclusion of children in community settings through training, on-site consultation, and professional development. She also teaches as adjunct faculty for Concordia University, St. Paul, Minnesota. She has worked in the special needs arena for the past fifteen years.

Dr. Laurie Glader is a developmental pediatrician at Children's Hospital in Boston where she directs the Cerebral Palsy Program and is a staff pediatrician with the Coordinated Care Services, a program designed to meet the needs of children with special health-care needs. Dr. Glader also teaches regularly at Harvard Medical School. Her work with public agencies includes New England SERVE, an organization that builds connections between state health departments, health-care organizations, community providers, and families. She is also the staff physician at the Cotting School, a school specializing in the education of children with a wide range of special health-care needs.